Dr. I. V. Hilliard

HOW TO WIN NO MATTER *where* YOU'RE STARTING FROM

LIVING
THE
MAXIMIZED
LIFE

NELSON BOOKS
A Division of Thomas Nelson Publishers
Since 1798
www.thomasnelson.com

Published by W Publishing Group, a Division of Thomas Nelson, Inc., P.O. Box 141000, Nashville, Tennessee, 37214.
www.thomasnelson.com

Nelson Books titles may be purchased in bulk for educational, business, fundraising, or sales promotional use. For information, please email SpecialMarkets@ThomasNelson.com.

All Scripture quotations, unless otherwise indicated, are taken from The King James Version of the Bible (KJV). Other Scripture references are from the following sources: The Amplified Bible (AMP), Old Testament. Copyright © 1962, 1964 by Zondervan Publishing House. Used by permission. The New King James Version (NKJV®), copyright 1979, 1980, 1982, Thomas Nelson, Inc., Publishers. The Holy Bible, New International Version (NIV). Copyright © 1973, 1978, 1984, International Bible Society. Used by permission of Zondervan Bible Publishers. New Living Translation (NLT) Holy Bible. New Living Translation copyright © 1996 by Tyndale Charitable Trust. Used by permission of Tyndale House Publishers.

Living the Maximized Life
Light Publications
P.O. Box 670167
Houston, TX 77267

ISBN: 1–5955–1015–4

Library of Congress Cataloging-in-Publication Data

Hilliard, I. V., 1952-
 Living the maximized life / I.V. Hilliard.
  p. cm.
 ISBN 1-59951-015-4
 1. Success—Religious aspects—Christianity. I. Title.
 BV4598.3.H55 2006
 248.4—dc22

2006015010

Printed in the United States of America
1 2 3 4 5 6 — 09 08 07 06

ACKNOWLEDGMENTS

I give honor and thanks to God for His Holy Spirit who is within me, teaching me, and guiding me through awesome projects like this, *Living the Maximized Life*.

Thanks to my beautiful wife, Dr. Bridget, for your continued support and dedication throughout the years. My life would not be as fulfilled and rewarding without you, my right hand.

Thanks to my children, Terry and Tina Egans, Jeff and Irishea Lewis, and Preashea Hilliard. You are following the course that God and your parents have developed for you. You make Dad very proud.

To my grandchildren, Ira-Emmanuel, Brionna, Ivan, and Jonathan— Big Daddy loves you.

Much love to my wonderful congregation of New Light Church World Outreach and Worship Centers in Houston (North, South, and East), Beaumont, and Austin, Texas. We have been through much together and conquered all. I love you all, and you are by far the best church in this world!

And last, but not least, thanks to Alison Howard, who has committed countless hours to make sure her pastor's book is nothing short of the very best.

CONTENTS

SECTION FOUR
The Mechanics for Maximizing Life

──── Introduction ────

Why *write a book like this?* This question always comes to mind when I sit down to start a labor of love. Other questions also bombard my mind:

- Will anybody read it?
- Hasn't enough been written on this subject?
- How long will it take to put my thoughts on paper?
- How many pages will the book be?
- Will anyone deem this book important enough to recommend it to others?
- Will this book become an invitation for critics to launch attacks against me?

I could go on, allowing the questions to build a wall of intimidation and chart a retreat from the keys of the word processor; but, as always, I choose to go with my heart and continue to write. But in order for me to begin and then complete this task, I must have a driving passion; otherwise, my life is much too busy to engage in some uninspiring enterprise. When I thought of what this book could do

for readers like you, a thrill and an excitement bubbled up in me. It compelled me to capture my God-inspired thoughts on maximizing life situations.

I am a student of human behavior, and I am always intrigued by people. Why do they behave the way they do? Further, I am even more curious about what motivates people in various life situations. I'm eager to know what guides their behavior. As a pastor for over three decades (at the time of this writing), I've dedicated my life to helping people live productive lives, lives that are beneficial to themselves and to those around them. My life's assignment has allowed me to observe the lives of people in all sorts of situations and dilemmas: some toxic, some taxing, some turbulent, and some triumphant. I want to see people like you experience God's best in life, and that makes my lifelong commitment to faith so substantive. The purpose of this book is to help you rise to a higher level of meaning and productivity in life.

Your life has tremendous value and purpose! When I write, I like to imagine my readers. I think about my audience and what this message of faith is capable of doing for them. When I write, I imagine that I am speaking to a seeker of knowledge and wisdom—just as I was years ago when I was so dissatisfied and so disappointed with my life. Somehow, I knew there was more. Somehow, I knew that better things were possible, but those things always seemed to elude me.

At that time, my mind was so conditioned for failure and frustration that consistently winning in life was literally unimaginable. Today, however, life is totally different. I'm living a fulfilled, happy life and pursuing my passion of ministry and helping people. I feel an obligation to tell you how my wife and I were able to rise from obscure and meager beginnings to the place where we now positively influ-

ence hundreds of thousands. We learned the keys to maximized living and have been sharing these principles with others for over twenty years. This book is that message, and its message is for you.

When most of us casually observe successful people, regardless of the arena, we overlook the price they paid to arrive at the success we admire. Because of our fairy-tale conditioning, we think, *Here is a person who was ushered into stardom on a flowery bed of ease*. The truth, in most cases, is that this is a person who endured hardships, who resisted the temptation to quit, who bucked the odds and overcame much opposition to achieve renown. It is only when the myths and misconceptions about success are dispelled that you can accept the truth: something better is possible for you. If others could learn how to win with the hand they were dealt in life, then you, too, can take the cards the dealer of the universe has dealt, and you can win. Unlike those fun card games in which you play against the dealer, in this game of life you are playing with a dealer who wants you to win. If you study your hand carefully, you will see clearly that your hand is not so bad, and with the right knowledge and passion, you, too, can be a winner.

Perhaps you are the seeker of knowledge and truth. You want to change your state in life. I have good news for you, my friend. I believe our meeting in the pages of this book is God-ordained, and I am eager to take you on a journey of personal growth to show you how I and many others have maximized life. No, you will not be a spectator on this journey; you will be a participant. When all is said and done, you will have in your possession the keys to open the doors you once thought were impassable.

Years ago I was invited by a client to go sailing on his midsize yacht. I had never been sailing and, quite frankly, I was excited about

the new adventure. For those of us who grew up in the ghettos of Houston, Texas, the thought of pleasure boating never entered our minds. Oh, I had some friends who owned small fishing boats, but I knew no one who owned a sailboat. Bright and early one Saturday morning, I met my client at the dock. I was ready to experience sailing. My friend began to explain the logistics and my part as the second half of our two-man crew. Crew? You mean I was part of the crew?

It was a startling reality check: on midsize sailing vessels, everyone is expected to pitch in and do his or her part, large or small, to make the journey safe and pleasurable. What I thought would be a simple, kick back, take-it-easy day of sailing with the wind and sea spray blowing in my face turned out to be a thrilling learning experience that gave me a deep appreciation for the skill involved in sailing. As you and I journey together over the waves of these next few pages, you will move from spectator to crewmember. When all is said and done, you will be equipped with the knowledge and ignited in the faith to maximize life's diverse and challenging situations.

Section One

The Methods for Maximizing Life

──── CHAPTER 1 ────

THE BELIEF IN MAXIMIZED LIVING

I t's the end of another counseling session, and I never cease to be amazed at the misguided expectations of most people concerning the quality of life in Christ. Quality of life is mostly a matter of choice and not always a matter of birth. Many people have a misconception that those who succeed and do well in life do so because they faced no challenges. The truth is just the opposite. Most people who succeed and experience a high quality of life do so by overcoming tremendous odds. Most of the people we admire have an extraordinary story, a narrative of maximizing life.

Maximizing life is a disciplined and quality choice to approach life with a positive, progressive, persistent attitude. Doing so allows one to overcome handicaps, hardships, and setbacks without bitterness, by choosing to embrace God's best. I have studied high achievers and observed successful people around me. There are common denominators among those I call "maximizers." Maximizers are individuals who possess the strength of character that enables them to keep believing, keep planning, keep thinking, and keep working to experience their full potential despite difficult conditions.

Another amazing misunderstanding many Christians and non-

Christians have is about trouble, tragedy, and misfortune. Some believe God sends the troubles, trials, and tribulations we face. Still others believe that if you are a Christian you should be exempt from all trouble. Unfortunately, a small group is in denial about the trouble issue and will say it does not exist. Oddly enough, these "extremes" are the majority, and very few people understand the true meaning of trouble.

The myths surrounding the trouble issue continue because of the religious taboo about questioning God. It is often said that one should never question God, but I believe that if I can ask God a question that He cannot answer, He can't be God. It is unfortunate that most well-meaning believers in the Christian faith think God is mysterious and operates on earth in mysterious ways. I hold to the position that God is not mysterious and He desires for man to know Him. If God wanted to be shrouded in mystery, why would He have allowed the Bible to be written, a document which tells His plans for the ages? No, my friend, God wants us to understand that He is a God of order. He even submits Himself to the order He has established. Therefore, our relationship with God should be full of confidence and predictability.

The Bible clearly addresses the "trouble in life" and the "adversity" questions. One of the greatest breakthroughs I had in my search to understand life was when I discovered that the will of God is not executed automatically on the earth. It requires man's invitation and participation. That's right! In order for the will of God to come to pass, mankind must be an active participant. Again, traditional religious thinking has been a barrier to sound knowledge, since it has deviated from Scripture. We are taught in the Scripture to reason, to study, and to understand the Word of God.

Here is a simple reasoning exercise to prove that the will of God does not automatically come to pass on the earth:

The Bible teaches in 2 Peter 3:9 that God does not want any people to perish and that all should repent. Further, the Bible teaches in John 3:16 that God sent Jesus to give His life for the whole world so that everyone might be saved. Based on these two passages of Scripture, it is the established and undeniable will of God for every person to be saved. But, will everyone be saved and no one be lost? The Bible clearly teaches that even though it is the will of God for all to be saved, some will not be saved and will unfortunately spend eternity in the lake of fire (Revelation 21:8). Those who will be lost will only be lost because they refused to receive the salvation and redemption that is so freely offered.

I rest my case. It is the will of God for all to be saved, but all will not be saved unless they do what is necessary to receive salvation. God's will only comes to pass with man's permission and man's participation.

Let's address the issue of adversity, trials, and troubles from a reasonable Scriptural perspective. As we search the pages of the Bible, we discover quickly that facing times of trouble is simply a part of human existence. The Bible is filled with passages, which demonstrate clearly that all are meant to face trouble in life.

These things I have spoken unto you, that in me ye might have peace. In the world ye shall have tribulation: but be of good cheer; I have overcome the world (John 16:33).

Since trouble seems inescapable, preparation for trouble is extremely important. Being a Christian is not an automatic exemption from trouble, but it is an assurance that we can expect divine help to

get us through our trouble. So many biblical characters who lived faithful and righteous lives still faced times of trouble and adversity. But because of their decisions to overcome the difficulties, they received supernatural (though not always spectacular) help and assistance from God. The following passages show us that God is committed to help His covenant people when trouble comes:

Many are the afflictions of the righteous: but the LORD *delivereth him out of them all (Psalm 34:19).*

Offer unto God thanksgiving; and pay thy vows unto the most High: And call upon me in the day of trouble: I will deliver thee, and thou shalt glorify me (Psalm 50:14-15).

Then they cry unto the LORD *in their trouble, and he saveth them out of their distresses. He sent his word, and healed them, and delivered them from their destructions (Psalm 107:19-20).*

Beloved, I wish above all things that thou mayest prosper and be in health, even as thy soul prospereth (3 John 2).

Christians must face the scriptural reality that life in Christ is not an automatic exemption from difficulties, hardships, and handicaps. When we face difficult, distasteful, disastrous times, we must choose to overcome them through faith in God. The maximized life is the life of the "overcomer." This is one who faces the less-than-optimal situations in life, and instead of throwing in the towel or buckling under and quitting, works through them to realize his dreams and full potential.

KEY STATEMENT: Real quality of life is determined by what you do in less-than-optimal situations and the way you fare under pain and pressure.

Careful study of those whom we admire in life reveals their success in overcoming tough situations. The biblical characters whom we hold in high esteem are those who maximized life's circumstances and lived life to the fullest.

Moses, the great leader of the Hebrews, had to overcome mistakes in judgment that could have derailed his destiny, but he had the strength of character to work through life's difficulties.

David, the hero and King of Israel, was indeed a maximizer. His life was filled with times of misfortune, disappointment, betrayal, and personal failure, yet he is still admired because he had the strength of character to work through life's difficulties.

Peter, the famous disciple of Jesus Christ, failed many times and faced what could have been disastrous situations, but he chose to persevere.

The list of biblical characters who faced troubled times—times that could have meant their demise—goes on and on. This is what makes the Bible so exciting—it is human; it is real.

The great apostle Paul writes to the church in Corinth to remind them that trouble is a part of life. More importantly, he tells them there is no trouble that they will face that someone else has not already encountered and overcome. "There hath no temptation taken you but such as is common to man: but God is faithful, who will not suffer you to be tempted above that ye are able; but will with the temptation also make a way to escape, that ye may be able to bear

it" (1 Corinthians 10:13). This ancient text continues to inspire the people of God and encourages us on our journey. Trouble never takes God by surprise, and for every troubled situation, God himself has devised a victorious plan of action.

If you study those in contemporary life who excel in their careers, you will always find underlying stories of their strength of character, which enabled them to overcome the less-than-optimal situations they faced. This reality along with the testimony of Scripture encourages us. It tells us that maximizing life is a critical choice we must all make.

Somehow, without a deep understanding of the Scripture at the time but with a resolve to do well in life, I adopted this maximizing mentality and attitude toward life. Though I grew up in a society that treated African-Americans as second-class citizens and swam through the undercurrents of prejudices, I was determined to succeed. I had a marvelous opportunity extended to me when I was hired as a computer operator trainee. This was long before the days of desktop and laptop computers, a time when most computer work was done on large "mainframes."

These mainframe computers were about the size of small automobiles and were housed in large heavily air-conditioned rooms. A Hispanic friend of mine recommended me for the job, and I was hired and given this opportunity even though I had no formal electronic data processing training. Most of the computer operators were either Hispanic or white and had graduated from a vocational school; I was the first African-American employee the company hired. I really wanted to do well because I appreciated the opportunity. I did not want to embarrass my friend who recommended me, and I felt I represented the African-American work ethic.

I took the position with the understanding that I would be evaluated after the ninety-day probationary period. If I could not show proficiency in operating the computer, then I would be let go. It was a risk, but coming from a manual labor job at a hardware supply company, I thought it was a risk worth taking. At least this job held future opportunities.

Unfortunately, my assigned supervisor did not share my enthusiasm or my dream of advancement in the computer industry. He was assigned to train me on the second shift, which ran from 3:00 p.m. to 11:00 p.m. My future, my livelihood, and my family depended on my success. But instead of teaching me the principles of data processing and training me on the operation of the computer, my supervisor assigned me to decollate the carbon sheets from the multipart paper. It was a tedious, non-skilled task in a little room, out of sight and away from the mainframe computer. To make matters worse, after several weeks he began to misrepresent me to the Data Processing Manager, saying that I was incompetent, slow, and not "catching on." That's right! He was not training me. He would hardly let me touch the computer. Yet he was misrepresenting my work. My dream was quickly turning into a nightmare.

I tried to be extra nice to my supervisor. I would work through my lunch break to finish my decollating chores before quitting time so that I could stand in the computer room, thinking that maybe he would explain something. I would ask questions, but I only received muttered responses. Wow! It sure looked like I was in a pickle. The clock was still ticking, counting down toward the end of my ninety-day probationary period. What was I to do? I could cry foul and prejudice, but that would only make me look like a troublemaker and I would be out the door for sure. I could just quit and save myself the

embarrassment of not being able to pass the test at the end of the probationary period. I could go back to the warehouse job; maybe they would hire me back. After all, I was a very good employee and they did not want me to leave their employment. Somehow, quitting was not an option. I did not know how I would overcome this obstacle to my success, but I knew something had to give. I prayed for guidance and kept doing my menial task. I kept my attitude positive and continued to be a good employee.

A few weeks into my probationary period, the late-night supervisor, who worked the 11:00 p.m. to 7:00 a.m. shift, pulled me aside and told me he wanted to talk. He told me in that very private conversation that he saw what was going on. He knew I was not being trained on the computer systems, and I was being misrepresented by my supervisor. He made an offer to help me, and it was one of the turning points in my data processing career. I probably would have never become a systems analyst if this opportunity had not been extended to me.

The late night supervisor offered to train me on his shift if I was willing to put forth the extra effort. I would have to work my regular shift from 3:00 p.m. to 11:00 p.m. and then go to the coffee shop just down the street from the company until shift change was completed. After the shift change, I could come back to work, not clock in, and learn. He would teach me the "ins and outs" of computer operations. It meant that I would work two shifts, but only get paid for one. Well, I saw this as God's answer to my dilemma. All I needed was the strength of character to organize my life and to discipline my thoughts. Only then could I see this as an opportunity to invest in myself.

A few of the other operators found out about what I was doing

and attempted to talk me out of it. They told me I should tell management about my supervisor. Remember that this all happened in the early 1970s when laws were not so favorable for the worker who cried foul. I ignored my comrades and persevered. In fact, I was enjoying the experience. The late night supervisor gave me his books from the vocational school he attended. He would highlight the significant chapters to accelerate my learning. It was fun—I have always loved learning.

On the day of reckoning at the end of the ninety-day probationary period, my supervisor—who had no knowledge of my late-night training program—told management how I was slow and unable to catch on. As we all stood around the computer, the faces of the managers were very grim as they began to prepare me for the exit speech, saying, "Not everyone has what it takes, but that doesn't mean that you can't succeed at something else." I should mention that my supervisor did not represent the attitude of the company at all. Well, the test was about to be administered. The test was straightforward: I would be given a sample job to run that would cover the full gambit of computer skills necessary to be an asset to the company.

The manager handed me the job. In those days we used punched cards. (Now that really dates me!) All eyes in the computer room were on me, but with confidence I stepped forward, read the instructions, made the necessary corrections to the control card, and began to run the job. You should have seen the look on my supervisor's face. I couldn't help but wink at him in his astonishment. The manager looked perplexedly at him as if to say, *But I thought you said he was incompetent?* I not only completed the task accurately and efficiently, but in record time. I was good, and I knew it! I had paid the price to maximize my situation!

I was praised by management. My supervisor finally came around and treated me with the respect that I deserved, and I was applauded by all of my coworkers. I thoroughly enjoyed working for that company, but I eventually moved to another firm and continued my career in data processing. With this same never-say-quit, do-what-it-takes-to-win attitude, I ultimately became a computer programmer and systems analyst without formal classroom instruction.

Remember who maximizers are.

KEY STATEMENT: Maximizers are those who possess the strength of character that enables them to keep believing, keep planning, keep thinking, and keep working to experience their full potential in the face of less-than-optimal conditions.

This is the simple hallmark of those who choose to succeed in life, whether that success is in business, in academic achievement, in ministry, or in relationships. In this life when you face less-than-optimal conditions and situations, you will either become a criticizer, a traumatizer, or a maximizer. The choice is all yours.

Criticizers choose to blame others for their own inability to succeed, finding fault with everything from their own upbringing to the government. Traumatizers are like criticizers with the added trait of trying to make everybody else's life miserable and unbearable by whining and complaining. They carry on this way with the misguided expectation that someone owes them something and, therefore, someone else should fix their problem. Maximizers, in contrast, bear down under pressure. Although they may feel like quitting, they

persevere with innovation until they achieve. Although maximizing career opportunities afforded me great pleasure, learning to optimize and maximize my marriage has given me the greatest satisfaction.

My wife and I had to make a decision to maximize our marriage instead of allowing the problems we faced to end in divorce. As of this writing, our marriage is thirty years strong, and we are both enjoying it to the fullest. Even though all is well today, it was not several years into our marriage. Far from it. We were both very young and immature when we married, and we each had our selfish reasons for marrying, hidden reasons that would later surface and become the catalyst for severe disappointment.

KEY STATEMENT: Like many couples who get married and face problems, we loved each other, but we lacked the interpersonal skills needed to build a healthy relationship.

After seeking counsel from other ministers with unfulfilled marriages, we found ourselves on a path to divorce that neither one of us wanted to travel. The turning point came when we both decided that we would look at God's plan for marriage, find an example of a good marriage to use as a pattern, drop our pride, learn to forgive, and work on building a relationship instead of destroying each other. It was not an overnight journey. The first three months were most challenging, but through it all God led us to the right people and the right information. Because our hearts were right, we built a strong marriage that is now a role model for many couples across the world. It's amazing what can be accomplished with the maximizing attitude.

My wife and I lead an incredible megachurch in Houston, Texas, that we founded in 1984. In the early days of the church ministry we faced trying, challenging times just about every month, but we were maximizers and chose to have strength of character. Such strength helped us continue to pray, to plan, to think, and to experience our full potential in the face of these less-than-optimal conditions. Instead of enjoying a quick increase in our flock at the outset of our ministry, we experienced a rapid decrease in membership: a decline of 92 percent in one week! We had to wade through times of limited resources, disloyal staff, abrupt displacement from our worship facility, transient membership, and unwarranted persecution. We could have quit, thrown in the towel, and blamed others, but we chose to maximize our situation.

We began with a dream, twenty-three members, and very limited resources. Today we see the fruit of our diligence and teach principles of maximized living to others. After years of faithfully applying the principles that we now teach others, our ministry has an international impact, hundreds of employees, a state-of-the-art media ministry, about four hundred acres of land, and over 750,000 square feet of building space. Through faith, the Spirit of God has taught us to overcome handicaps, hardships, and difficulties to build a megachurch ministry from the ground up.

All of these testimonials were written to encourage you on your journey to becoming a maximizer. You can accomplish so much more. You have so much more to give to your family and so much more to offer in your profession. Your best days are ahead.

While writing this book our city, Houston, Texas, has become the caretaker of thousands of displaced residents from New Orleans, Louisiana. More than most, these people must face the future with

maximizers' attitudes, choosing to make the most out of less-than-optimal situations. I met with several religious leaders from New Orleans who at first seemed in a state of depression and devastation. These pastors had lost their congregations, their church facilities, and their personal assets. We cannot imagine the sense of devastation and despair one is subjected to in a situation like this. Those who were positive and optimistic were the leaders who did not let the floodwaters wash away their dreams. I shared with them that they should establish a church fellowship here in Houston to accommodate their displaced membership. I could clearly see their eyes light up with hope as their dreams were revived.

The Bible unequivocally teaches that God is not a respecter of persons; therefore, every covenant believer has a right to expect the divine intervention necessary to bring deliverance from their trouble. This intervention may not always be at the spectacular level of the miraculous, but it might come through the divine orchestration of events working together to effect outcome. Every person in the family of God has the right to expect the blessings of God, the favor of God, and divine assistance to help through tough times.

People so often shortchange themselves. They rob themselves of the maximizer position through self condemnation and flawed religious beliefs about God. I have good news that can dispel the myth that the God of the Bible is some cosmic bully waiting to settle the score with you for your misbehavior. The biblical truth is that He is a God of love and forgiveness, and your repentance sets the stage for your fresh start and the favor of God. Sincere repentance causes one to become truly sorrowful. Only when you truly repent of your disobedience will you be in line for God's best. God's love and forgiveness are almost too good to be true because He will forget your past

and bless you as though none of your misbehavior had ever happened.

In Matthew 20:1-16, Jesus tells a story to illustrate the mercy of God. He talks about a landowner who hired workers at different times of the day, agreeing with each group to pay a day's wage. He hired a group in the morning, another group at noon, and still another group just before quitting time. At the end of the day, he paid them all the same day's wage, regardless of the length of their employment. Jesus told this simple story to emphasize that no matter when you establish a covenant relationship with God, you can count on Him keeping His Word.

> *But when the first came, they supposed that they should have received more; and they likewise received every man a penny. And when they had received it, they murmured against the goodman of the house, saying, "These last have wrought but one hour, and thou hast made them equal unto us, which have borne the burden and heat of the day." But he answered one of them, and said, "Friend, I do thee no wrong: didst not thou agree with me for a penny? Take that thine is, and go thy way: I will give unto this last, even as unto thee. Is it not lawful for me to do what I will with mine own? Is thine eye evil, because I am good?" So the last shall be first, and the first last: for many be called, but few chosen (Matthew 20:10-16).*

At this point in our journey it would be good to examine yourself to determine if you have established a relationship with God based on His Word. We hear the Christian term "salvation," but often we cannot relate to it. Let me attempt to make God's amazing plan crystal clear in a concise explanation. God created the world perfect in

every way and gave the earth to man to control and manage, with the stipulation that he must obey Him. Mankind's representative was the first man, Adam, who was warned about the consequences of disobedience. These consequences would affect the entire human race. Adam chose to disobey God, committed "sin," and opened the door for the consequences of disobedience, which were hardship, loss of control of the earth, and eternal death and separation from God. God devised a plan for mankind's restoration based on a simple promise: because of one man's failure, the consequences were felt by all; and through one man's uncompromising obedience, the consequences could be eradicated for all.

Jesus Christ, the Son of God, became a man so He could live as mankind's representative and pay the ultimate price for mankind's sins and failure through Adam. So Jesus lived the perfect life and, therefore, should not have been subject to the consequence of sin, but He died as an innocent man taking the place of all of the guilty. God, validating the process, miraculously raised Jesus from the dead and settled this issue forever. He declared that if any man will accept the substitute paid (the life of Jesus), believing and surrendering one's life to God, the consequences of sin would be waived and forgiven. The acceptance can be communicated through a simple prayer based on this simple understanding of God's plan of salvation. "That if thou shalt confess with thy mouth the Lord Jesus, and shalt believe in thine heart that God hath raised him from the dead, thou shalt be saved" (Romans 10:9).

Here is a simple prayer of repentance and salvation that will put you in the family of God and position you to live the abundant, maximized life:

Dear God, I know that without Jesus I am lost. I believe Your Word that Jesus came to give His life for me so that I would not be lost. I believe that Jesus lived, died in my place, and was raised from the dead. I choose now to turn my back on my old way of living, and I receive Your forgiveness of all my sins and wrongdoings. Jesus, I give You the throne of my heart, and from this day forward I choose to please You with my life. Now, fill me with Your power and strength to live a life that is pleasing in Your sight. In the name of Jesus, I pray. Amen.

As you prayed that prayer all of heaven stopped, and the angels began to rejoice over your commitment to God: "Likewise, I say unto you, there is joy in the presence of the angels of God over one sinner that repenteth" (Luke 15:10).

Although you could not feel it, your spirit became alive to God, and now you will begin to experience the Spirit of God leading you in life through the inner witness of peace. Wow! You are a part of the family of God, and it's time to learn how to maximize life!

CHAPTER 2

THE BLESSING FROM MAXIMIZERS

That ye be not slothful, but followers of them who through faith and patience inherit the promises (Hebrews 6:12).

Simply put, this Scripture says the Lord inspires us through the success and productivity of others. So many times in the Bible the people of God were instructed to gain strength from the lives and testimonies of others. This chapter highlights several historical and contemporary maximizers. Some of these maximizers are in the Bible. Some I have read about, and others I know personally.

People often ask why we should study the Bible, because to some it seems an outdated and antiquated book of rules and regulations not relevant to contemporary life. These impressions are misguided; I have discovered the Bible to be a source of divine truths and principles that are relevant for every generation. This ancient text contains stories, principles, and prophecies for the future. We study characters in the Bible so that we may learn from their experiences with God and life. We study the doctrines of the Bible so that we may

learn and understand the order of God and the ways of God, which in turn cause us to have more confidence in God.

We study the Bible because it exposes a dimension of reality that is not visible to the natural eye—the realm of the spirit. "For whatsoever things were written aforetime were written for our learning, that we through patience and comfort of the scriptures might have hope" (Romans 15:4).

There is more to life than what you and I can see and touch. You know this to be true, since we all take for granted the existence of invisible radio and television waves. So, you must agree that in this life there are invisible elements all around us. Read any physics book or microbiology book and it will detail these invisible realities. So it is with the Bible. It is a book that explains the invisible realm of the spirit, exposing the spiritual laws that are at work on earth.

"For by him were all things created, that are in heaven, and that are in earth, visible and invisible, whether they be thrones, or dominions, or principalities, or powers: all things were created by him, and for him" (Colossians 1:16). When man began to understand more about the invisible laws of physics, he also began to maximize life on earth through inventions and innovations. When scientists began to learn more about the world of microbiology, they also began to develop more effective medicines and remedies for viruses and diseases. So it is when men come to understand the spiritual laws that affect life. They learn how to maximize quality of life. A study of the Bible and the lives of those in the Bible is not casual reading, but it is research undertaken to understand principles for maximized living.

In Hebrews 6:12, there is a powerful spiritual principle worth examining: "That ye be not slothful, but followers of them who

through faith and patience inherit the promises." Simply stated, this passage instructs the student of life to study the lives of those who have maximized life and are walking in the promises of God. The Greek word for "follow" is the root from which we get the English word "imitate." That's right; we are instructed by Scripture to imitate the character traits and principles of those who have been successful. Now we will look at the lives of both historical and contemporary individuals who made the choice to maximize life.

KEY STATEMENT: Maximizers, like all people, eventually reach a "breaking point," but instead of breaking down they break through, which is a matter of choice.

You can decide right now to completely change your life, using a different attitude and a different approach while facing the same circumstances you now encounter. Your attitude can change based on the conviction you have in God's Word. It is a matter of choice. This is not denial; it is a choice, and the Bible says that we have the right to choose. We cannot control the trouble that comes into our lives because if we had it our own way, we would not have any trouble.

KEY STATEMENT: We can't control the trouble that comes but we can control our response to the trouble.

If we respond properly to the challenges in life, we won't have that trouble long because we can overcome by faith. Deuteronomy

30 tells us that God sets before us life and death and we should choose life. "I call heaven and earth to record this day against you, that I have set before you life and death, blessing and cursing: therefore choose life, that both thou and thy seed may live" (v.19). You must decide for yourself to choose life. You have to decide that you are going to choose the path of the blessing. Again, it is a matter of choice. When distasteful, potentially devastating, and discomforting situations occur, you have to decide what you are going to be and who you are going to become. Are you going to be traumatized, paralyzed, and victimized, or are you going to maximize? It is your choice. Life isn't static; it's dynamic. You can let the issues of life paralyze you, which will be an emotional and spiritual "end point" for your whole life. For instance, if you are turned down for financing on a car, don't be afraid; go and apply again at a later date. If you are turned down for a mortgage, don't allow yourself to be so embarrassed that you never try again. Do you really want to live in that rental property for the rest of your life? Perhaps you couldn't go to college because your family did not have any money and you did not want to go into debt. You can still win. It's not too late to pursue that college degree. With the explosion of community colleges all over America, it is also possible to get your degree while holding down a full-time job.

You may have married an immature person who did not value you or appreciate your qualities. Maybe the relationship ended in a divorce. Whatever your current status is, don't choose to be paralyzed and live the rest of your life as a single, angry, and disgruntled person.

As a result of difficult situations, you can allow yourself to become traumatized. People are traumatizers when they choose to

make everyone else suffer for what they have experienced. These are the people who dump on others about what happened to them every time you talk to them. After a while, every time you see that traumatized person's phone number flash across the Caller ID, you don't answer the phone. Don't be that person on the other end of the line.

You can be victimized and live your life blaming that situation for everything else that happened. Today, New Light Church could still be a little congregation on Jensen Drive on the north side of Houston, twenty years after God told me to build a ministry of 18,000. I could still be saying what the Lord promised twenty years ago didn't happen because 92 percent of the membership left in one day, and I blamed my failure on those who left. In the midst of apparent failure, my wife and I chose to make the most of that unpleasant situation. You can let a situation victimize you, and you can go through the rest of your life talking about what could have been if something had not happened. Even though something negative may have happened, you must choose to maximize.

KEY STATEMENT: A maximizer plays with the hand he has been dealt and chooses to win with that hand.

You, too, can make that choice, believing the hand you have been dealt—that is, the situation you face—is one with which you can still win.

Recently, I read a true story about three guys who had a paint company that was not doing well. As a result, two of the partners bailed out of the company, leaving the third with all the debt and almost at the point of bankruptcy. So, the third guy began to ask the

customers and other people who were around him why they didn't buy more paint from him. The people said, "We don't like your colors. We want paint that we can mix and match in order to make colors we like." So, this third guy, by the name of Sherwin, came up with an idea that he took to his banker, Mr. Williams. He showed Mr. Williams his idea, and Mr. Williams thought it was such an innovative plan that he said, "Look, I am not going to let the bank do it; I'll do it personally." Now we have Sherwin-Williams™ paint covering the earth.

J. C. Penney is another example. He was fifty-five years old and facing bankruptcy—seven million dollars in the hole. He came up with an idea for a top-of-the-line department store. The idea blossomed, and he subsequently built an empire.

You must understand that you can turn situations around and success can be achieved. No matter what handicap you think you might have that can hinder your victory, you are only limited as much as you allow yourself to be limited.

Some of you who are close to my age may remember a famous football game played on November 8, 1970. The New Orleans Saints were losing to the Detroit Lions by two points. With two seconds on the clock, Tom Dempsey, a man born with no right hand and only half a foot, kicked the longest field goal ever recorded, sixty-three yards. This went down in the record book because he did not let his troubles impose limits on him.

You may be African-American. So what? There may be racial profiling, prejudices, and disadvantages. So what? Have you noticed that non-African-Americans do not always succeed? Being non-African-American is not a guarantee that you are going to win in life.

Stop using as an excuse that tired phrase, "They won't give a brother a break."

KEY STATEMENT: A covenant relationship with Jesus guarantees you
your break.

In the book of Ephesians, the great apostle Paul encourages the saints of God that the supernatural will of God is to do the unimaginable. "Now unto him that is able to do exceeding abundantly above all that we ask or think, according to the power that worketh in us" (Ephesians 3:20).

At this point it should be crystal clear that God is willing to do even more than you can dream of if you will just make the choice to win. He is ready, but will you choose to win? You have an opportunity to say, "I am not going to get stuck in this situation. This situation I have been handed is not what I like, but I am not going to get stuck in it. This situation is not what I expected, it's not what I planned, but I can move beyond this point because maximizers move beyond the point of breakdown and they break through."

Let's look at a couple of examples of maximizers in the Bible. There is a beautiful story told in Genesis 37–45 about a young man named Joseph, the son of Jacob. He was greatly favored by his father, which caused his brothers to become viciously jealous. His brothers conspired to kill him, but instead sold him to a traveling slave caravan. Despite this brutal beginning, Joseph ended up maximizing his life. He was a slave in Potiphar's house, but he worked diligently and became the head slave. "How?" you may ask. His secret was no secret at all: he did not allow himself to become bitter. Potiphar's wife lied

about Joseph, causing him to be thrown into prison, but he still managed to rise to the top. He did not let another negative situation get him down. He persevered again and was promoted to the chief of the prisoners.

It was in prison that a divine connection took place, and God's help caused him to be favored by those on the king's staff. One day when the king needed a dream interpreted, his staff member remembered Joseph and introduced him to the king. The king became so impressed with Joseph's wisdom that he promoted Joseph to prime minister. What an incredible story of maximizing a distasteful situation. Despite all that was done against him, Joseph eventually saw his dreams come true.

A more contemporary story is that of Malachi Johnson of Houston, Texas. Malachi Johnson is truly a maximizer. He works to help ministries all over America maximize their potential by advising them on the legal aspects of ministry. After being at New Light Church for a mere five months, Malachi and his family experienced a tragic turn of events, one that could have wrecked their lives forever. On July 19, 1996, while returning home from dinner, Malachi's vehicle was struck by a drunk driver who ran a traffic light. This horrific accident left Malachi unconscious and his vehicle crushed. A couple of hours after the collision, the terrible incident also caused the death of his wife of eleven years. Malachi was left to raise his two young daughters, Alyssa and Britney, ages seven and four, as a single parent. Malachi faced many emotions that could have crippled him for life, causing him to be angry at God and bitter toward others. During the four days he was hospitalized after the accident, he chose to forgive the driver for what the man had taken from Malachi's family.

Malachi made the crucial choice to make the most out of life and move on. He continued to raise his girls and pursued God's plan for his life. With the help of relatives, friends, and the spiritual support of the church, the Johnson family overcame what could have been most devastating. After a time of successfully raising his family, Malachi wanted to be married again and have his girls grow up with the nurturing of a mother's touch. In January 2000, while in Dallas on a blind date arranged by a friend, he met Harlene and immediately knew she was "the one." Malachi and Harlene were engaged after a nine-month courtship and married on June 2, 2001. Today, both Harlene and Malachi are members of the New Light team. Harlene works with the Community and Facility Development Department and is President of Light Commerce Credit Union. She also oversees the HUD grant for Faith Village Senior Apartments. Malachi serves as General Counsel to both the New Light Church and the Church Legal Resource Center, which helps churches and pastors across America with all the legal aspects of ministry. It is wonderful to see a fulfilled family working together in the kingdom of God. An event that could have soured his life forever was conquered and overcome by faith. Malachi and the Johnson family are maximizers, living life to its fullest.

In Romans 12:2 we are told that we have to renew our minds with the Word of God. When we renew our minds, we understand clearly that the will of God is not necessarily what you see people experience. That's right! The will of God is not based on what people experience. It is based only on what the Bible says. You must understand that if the will of God is going to come to pass in your life, you have to renew your mind and do what God says in order to bring His will to pass in your situation.

KEY STATEMENT: Often people give up too quickly, thinking their situation must be what God wants for them. Always know that God's will for your life is that you prosper, be in good health, overcome your difficulties, and most of all live an abundant life.

Beloved, I wish above all things that thou mayest prosper and be in health, even as thy soul prospereth (3 John 2).

For whatsoever is born of God overcometh the world: and this is the victory that overcometh the world, even our faith (1 John 5:4).

The thief cometh not, but for to steal, and to kill, and to destroy: I am come that they might have life, and that they might have it more abundantly (John 10:10).

Things don't always work out as you plan, but that does not mean they can't work out. Many people don't realize that Adam and Eve were maximizers, but they truly were. They experienced failure after making a tragic mistake, just like so many of us have failed. After Adam and Eve sinned, awful consequences were unleashed, but God made Eve a promise that she would have a son—a child who would bruise the serpent's head. She must have been really excited since she vowed that one day she would get even with the devil for deceiving her.

In Genesis 4:1, when Eve gave birth to the first boy, she declared, "I have gotten a man from the LORD." In other words, "All right devil, it's on now. I am ready for you now. God promised me a man, and I got a man child." That was her joy. She then had another boy.

Things seemed to be on the right track once again. But instead of these boys bringing her victory, they brought her despair. One killed the other, which is certainly not what she was expecting. She expected to get even with the devil. She expected that the boys would bruise the serpent's head. To the contrary, one killed the other and the murderer was cursed by God. It did not work out the way she wanted. Despite such persistent difficulty, the Bible tells us that Adam knew his wife again and they had another son, Seth. Eve did not stop trying to win, and eventually she did!

Let's look at another contemporary maximizer whose story will inspire you to be thankful and persevere regardless of what unexpected misfortune comes your way. On any given day you will see Sterling Armstead going about his work assignments as a staff member of New Light Church. Sterling has been a member of New Light Church for nine years. He is an inspiration to all with whom he comes in contact. After serving in the U.S. Navy for more than two and a half years, Sterling was released with a medical discharge. He began to experience severe swelling in his legs, and, after a battery of tests, he was the second person ever to be diagnosed with neurosarcodosis, a deterioration of the spinal cord that left him paralyzed. In 1989 at the young age of thirty-two, Sterling was told that he would never walk again. This could have meant the end of his dreams for a life of happiness and fulfillment.

After spending a long time in Independence Hall Rehabilitation Institute, Sterling emerged with a new zeal and determination to make the most of life. He chose not to blame God or drown himself in self-pity. To the contrary, Sterling chose to maximize his situation. He took life by the horns, and with determination and the help of God, Sterling now functions as a very independent man. His techni-

cal computer skills are much sought after, and he is only one course away from receiving an Associate's degree in Computer Networking. Sterling is an integral part of New Light's MIS department, an active church member, and a graduate of the Light Bible Institute and the Ministry Development Institute. Sterling drives himself, works over forty hours a week, and attends weekly worship services and Church-In-Action Bible studies. What an incredible man! Sterling Armstead maintains his faith in God. He knows that the power of God can reverse the disease that crippled him, but until then he chooses to maximize life and live life to the fullest.

KEY STATEMENT: Don't let anyone convince you that you cannot succeed and overcome adversity.

You have to play with the hand you have been dealt and know that hand is good enough to win. You win by acting on the principles of success found in the Word of God. "And be not conformed to this world: but be ye transformed by the renewing of your mind, that ye may prove what is that good, and acceptable, and perfect, will of God" (Romans 12:2).

Renewing the mind is a multifaceted process that involves three major components: consideration, education, and saturation. Consideration comes first. In order to embrace the mind-renewing process, you must first consider the facts and truths that are set before you; the Word of God and the real-life situations prove that every tragedy in life does not have to end in failure. The consideration phase is the moment when you look at life from a different perspective saying, "Oh, yes, it must be possible to overcome difficult

situations and maximize life, because I have seen that it is promised in the Word of God and there are people who are doing it."

The next component of the mind-renewing process is education. Accurate information is essential in the mind-transformation process.

KEY STATEMENT: Information empowers and equips you to win in life. It is not enough for someone to tell you that you should win; someone needs to instruct you on how to win in life.

That is what maximizers will do. Maximizers do not hang around losers so that they can develop excuses for being where they are. They seek winners, and they sit at their feet to learn principles for winning.

Finally, there is the component of repetitious saturation. Saturation means a diligent commitment to the process. We bring our old inferior thinking into the kingdom of God, and it must be overpowered with the new information. A casual approach to renewing the mind will yield very few results; however, more time spent absorbing spiritual truths and principles leads to greater transformation. Greater transformation leads to greater acceleration toward a maximized life.

CHAPTER 3

THE BLUEPRINT FOR MAXIMIZED LIVING

As a teenager I was always fascinated by blueprints. My brother worked as a draftsman, and I was awed at the details that went into a blueprint. It was a way of communicating information visually so the ideas of an architect could become a reality. The Bible is like a blueprint in that it contains detailed principles that will produce predetermined results again and again.

KEY STATEMENT: Unlike some religions, which teach acceptance of and surrender to life's mishaps, the Bible encourages a purposeful strategy to transform distasteful situations.

Understanding that the Bible is a book of life principles and strategies, and not just good ancient literature, gives a better appreciation of those truths. "All Scripture is given by inspiration of God, and is profitable for doctrine, for reproof, for correction, for instruction in righteousness" (2 Timothy 3:16).

The teachings of the Bible clearly show that God wants us to live a fulfilled and victorious life, overcoming all the trouble and obstacles that come our way. Victory over hardships and setbacks is a believer's spiritual entitlement, but it is not automatic. We must learn to make accurate, quality choices to get the most out of life. Choosing to live the maximized life is based on principles contained in the Scriptures. In this section of the book I want to share several exciting maximizing principles with you, along with testimonies of their impact in real-life situations.

In order to walk in any biblical truth, there are four mandatory elements. First, there must be a *revelation*, an understanding at the comprehension level of the individual. Second, there must be a *role model*. We must see that revealed truth lived out in the lives of others. It is still the consistent order of God to teach us and to train us by example. Third, there must be a *regimen of faith*; that is, a systematic application of the truths so that the promised results can be reproduced again and again. Fourth, there must be a *righteous resolve*, which is the Godly reason for the application of the principle. The truths presented in this section meet the biblical criteria for principles to live by in that these are principles in both precept and example, all with multiple biblical references.

Developing a "blueprint for maximized living" is imperative because it is the will of God for us to plan and develop strategies for living. Jesus taught this in the Gospel of Luke 14:28-32. This passage offers both practical and spiritual wisdom.

For which of you, intending to build a tower, sitteth not down first, and counteth the cost, whether he have sufficient to finish it? Lest haply, after he hath laid the foundation, and is not able to finish it, all

that behold it begin to mock him, saying, "This man began to build, and was not able to finish." Or what king, going to make war against another king, sitteth not down first, and consulteth whether he be able with ten thousand to meet him that cometh against him with twenty thousand? Or else, while the other is yet a great way off, he sendeth an ambassage, and desireth conditions of peace.

One of the many reasons people fail is because they don't plan to win. Not only do you need a purpose in your heart to win, but you also need a plan. Therefore, when you are developing a strategy, it is important to know the foundational principle of biblical success: "This book of the law shall not depart out of thy mouth; but thou shalt meditate therein day and night, that thou mayest observe to do according to all that is written therein: for then thou shalt make thy way prosperous, and then thou shalt have good success" (Joshua 1:8).

When understood clearly, the principles from the Word of God can change the way you view life. In fact, I think that once you seek truths sincerely and continue following those truths, transformation is bound to take place. "Then said Jesus to those Jews which believed on him, 'If ye continue in my word, then are ye my disciples indeed; and ye shall know the truth, and the truth shall make you free' " (John 8:31-32).

KEY STATEMENT: Your maximizing strategy must include an understanding of the perceived limitations and truth of the spiritual laws for success.

Limitations are only temporary. What limits you today may not be a limitation in the future. We don't deny there are limitations, but

we know they are only temporary. Most people are unable to adopt a maximizer's attitude because they face limited resources, limited knowledge, limited opportunity, and limited credentials. But all the things that are limited are subject to change. You may be facing limited resources today, but that does not mean it is always going to be so. You may be facing limited opportunities today, but that does not mean that doors will always be closed in the future.

KEY STATEMENT: Your whole attitude will change when you understand that limitations are temporary.

Those who choose to maximize their circumstances in life do so because they see limitations and discomforting situations as temporary obstacles, mere detours on the road to success.

KEY STATEMENT: Limitations in life are invisible barriers that intimidate the imagination and paralyze your thinking, shutting down the creative process, causing you to accept the present state as the apex of what is possible.

A limitation suggests that progress beyond the current point is impossible! Jesus pushed people, however, to challenge the perceived limitations that restricted them from experiencing new levels of living. Limitations, like other problems, become "wake-up calls" to our divine creativity and ingenuity! Viewed in this way, they become opportunities rather than obstacles.

1. LIMITED RESOURCES CAN ALWAYS BE OVERCOME.

There are several scriptural accounts where limited resources seem to be a hindrance to success. On the occasion of the feeding of the five thousand, what seemed to be a shortage became a surplus.

KEY STATEMENT: I never allow a lack of resources to interfere with my vision.

I have confidence that whatever I need already exists on the earth. All that needs to happen is for God to arrange the right people to make the right connections to meet a need. Careful study of the Scriptures shows that God gives you more on your way than He does before you get started.

2. LIMITED KNOWLEDGE CAN ALWAYS BE OVERCOME.

Limited knowledge is only a temporary state that lasts until knowledge is directly acquired through partnership. We live at a time when information about nearly any subject is at your fingertips through the Internet. You must always remember that there is someone who knows what you don't know, but need to know. Further, those who know what you need to know are always willing to offer their knowledge and expertise at a price. You are only limited in knowledge during the time it takes for you to acquire the knowledge yourself or employ those with the knowledge you need. Even Moses respected this truth. When he needed a guide to assist him in the wilderness, he contracted a man named Hobab to serve as his scout. This story is recorded in the book of Numbers 10:29-31. The moral of the story is this:

KEY STATEMENT: Never back away from a challenging opportunity because you lack the knowledge. You can always acquire knowledge.

---

3. LIMITED OPPORTUNITIES CAN ALWAYS BE OVERCOME.

Limited opportunities are only a temporary state until the favor of God opens a door of opportunity. Opportunity is the right of every giver because it is the blessing promised for obedience in the area of liberal giving. Manifested opportunity in life is our covenant right! Look at these two awesome promises about God raising up natural help when we give:

> "Bring ye all the tithes into the storehouse, that there may be meat in mine house, and prove me now herewith," saith the LORD of hosts, "if I will not open you the windows of heaven, and pour you out a blessing, that there shall not be room enough to receive it" (Malachi 3:10).

> And God is able to make all grace abound toward you; that ye, always having all sufficiency in all things, may abound to every good work (2 Corinthians 9:8).

KEY STATEMENT: When my heart is right toward God and my desire is to please God, I obligate God to bring me into the company of the people I need to know who are critical to my success and destiny.

---

4. LIMITED CREDENTIALS CAN ALWAYS BE OVERCOME.

Limited credentials are only a temporary state until exceptional performance is recognized or favor shines upon you. It is interesting how I developed expertise and was recognized for my ability in areas where I had no formal training. In the data processing arena, I was never supposed to rise above a Computer Operator Supervisor because I lacked the credentials to be a Computer Programmer. The Computer Programmer job description stated that a bachelor's degree was required. Without one, it said, you should not even bother to apply for the job. Well, I'm a maximizer and I wanted to become a programmer, so I worked with the programmers and asked them questions. Before long I learned several computer programming languages and began to write programs. I had thoroughly proven my diligence and excellence as a Computer Operator Supervisor, and even though I did not have a bachelor's degree, my track record of being an excellent performer and producer was accepted as credentials for the programming opportunity. Further, my excellent performance as a young programmer and systems analyst became my credentials that earned me respect among my peers.

Spiritual laws must be a part of the believer's "overcoming" strategy. Laws work for those who work the laws. When I am functioning in agreement with a natural law, I am guaranteed certain results. So it is with spiritual laws. My efforts will not be in vain because a law works for those who work the law. There are seven laws that must be mastered in order to consistently maximize life situations.

1. THE LAW OF PERSPECTIVE

You must create and maintain a vision of where you are going before you get there. The Bible has multitudes of Scriptures admonishing

believers to control their visual focus. Seeing your future from God's perspective is critical to accurate management of your mind. The term "vision" has the most dynamic and multi-faceted meaning. It means both natural visual perception and spiritual internal vision (or imagination).

KEY STATEMENT: The law of perspective says you tend to believe what you can see and focus on consistently.

God taught Abram to maximize his potential as he pursued possession of the Promised Land. Carefully consider God's instruction to Abram concerning his mental focus:

And the LORD said unto Abram, after that Lot was separated from him, "Lift up now thine eyes, and look from the place where thou art northward, and southward, and eastward, and westward: For all the land which thou seest, to thee will I give it, and to thy seed for ever. And I will make thy seed as the dust of the earth: so that if a man can number the dust of the earth, then shall thy seed also be numbered. Arise, walk through the land in the length of it and in the breadth of it; for I will give it unto thee" (Genesis 13:14-17).

Abram is instructed to look from where he is to where he wants to go. This simple principle of focus will transform your life as you immerse yourself in images of the new you in possession of your faith's desires.

Perspective has to do with the deeply rooted meaning that you give to life's circumstances based on the way you internally process

information. A person's perspective becomes a person's reality. A maximizer chooses to look at life from a winning perspective, not from a losing one.

KEY STATEMENT: A maximizer is not a person who denies reality, but is a person who chooses to focus on the possible positive outcome and works toward that end.

The Christian who operates in faith chooses to be very optimistic about even the worst situation, knowing that attitude and behavior are products of perspective. We must look at life assured that we have a commitment from God to help us successfully navigate life's challenges, no matter how difficult they might be, no matter how dangerous, and no matter how distasteful.

2. THE LAW OF PASSION

The law of passion says that when you pursue something with all your might you always find the initiative and sense of urgency to accomplish the goal.

This law is normally violated by those who are "laid back" and make excuses for their lack of success. The Scriptures that support this law are too numerous to list in this discussion, but here are two key examples:

Wherefore seeing we also are compassed about with so great a cloud of witnesses, let us lay aside every weight, and the sin which doth so easily beset us, and let us run with patience the race that is set before

us, looking unto Jesus the author and finisher of our faith; who for the joy that was set before him endured the cross, despising the shame, and is set down at the right hand of the throne of God (Hebrews 12:1-2).

Jesus Christ had an insatiable desire to liberate humanity through His sacrificial death on the cross. Careful study of His life shows that while praying in the garden of Gethsemane, Jesus struggled with obeying God at this level. The Bible clearly says that Jesus requested that the "cup of sorrows" would pass from Him. Yet, when He reconsidered and developed a passion to succeed, it produced the endurance and strength of character to do what was extremely difficult. Here is another Scripture to support the law of passion as a key to success.

"Blessed are they which do hunger and thirst after righteousness: for they shall be filled" (Matthew 5:6). You and I will be filled, satisfied at the level of our hunger and thirst for the things of God. Hunger and thirst are synonymous terms for passion. I really like this passage because of the guarantee that is incorporated in the text. If you and I hunger and thirst for righteousness, then we can rest assured that God will empower us to obtain the righteous objectives we are passionate about. Learning how to stir up a hunger and a thirst for something is the key.

I often tell the story of a great place in Palm Springs, California, that serves the best chocolate cake I have ever eaten. This restaurant serves a giant slice of delicious, melt-in-your-mouth cake with ice cream, which I think is the best chocolate dessert. This is a four-layer cake, and each layer has chocolate nuggets in the chocolate filling

between each layer. Oh, did I tell you about the walnuts? That's right; walnuts are sprinkled throughout the chocolate filling. Every year I go there just for the dessert, and every year I leave extremely satisfied.

I went into that lengthy explanation to illustrate a point. As I described the dessert in detail, you began to think about what it would taste like. You probably would like to know the name of the place, especially if you are a chocolate-cake lover. My satisfied recollection created a hunger and thirst in you. So, in order to become passionate about the pursuit of a maximized life, you must hear testimonies of those who are living maximized lives. Their testimonies stimulate you to follow in their footsteps.

3. THE LAW OF PRIORITY

The law of priority says what you choose as the object of your focus, coupled with arranging your life to give it maximum attention, increases your chances for success in that area. Many Scriptures teach the importance of prioritizing and engaging in focused living to produce excellence. Many passages encourage putting the kingdom of God first and arranging your life so that you will overcome whatever you are facing.

KEY STATEMENT: Put God, His principles, and spiritual law first in your life, and success will follow.

Brethren, I count not myself to have apprehended: but this one thing I do, forgetting those things which are behind, and reaching forth unto

those things which are before, I press toward the mark for the prize of the high calling of God in Christ Jesus (Philippians 3:13-14).

But seek ye first the kingdom of God, and his righteousness; and all these things shall be added unto you (Matthew 6:33).

The light of the body is the eye: if therefore thine eye be single, thy whole body shall be full of light" (Matthew 6:22).

The law of priority reveals the power of focused effort and discipline, which lead to skill and mastery. Understanding how to set priorities in life is critical if one wants to develop and implement a strategy to maximize life's opportunities. Things that are highly valued and yield the most desirable results must be given priority.

4. THE LAW OF PETITION

The law of petition is quite simple: God will grant me that for which I pray.

Give not that which is holy unto the dogs, neither cast ye your pearls before swine, lest they trample them under their feet, and turn again and rend you. Ask, and it shall be given you; seek, and ye shall find; knock, and it shall be opened unto you (Matthew 7:6-7).

And Jabez was more honourable than his brethren: and his mother called his name Jabez, saying, "Because I bare him with sorrow." And Jabez called on the God of Israel, saying, "Oh that thou wouldest bless me indeed, and enlarge my coast, and that thine hand might be with me, and that thou wouldest keep me from evil, that it

may not grieve me!" And God granted him that which he requested (1 Chronicles 4:9-10).

Call unto me, and I will answer thee, and show thee great and mighty things, which thou knowest not (Jeremiah 33:3).

Isn't it incredible that if we call on Him, He will answer?

And this is the confidence that we have in him, that, if we ask any thing according to his will, he heareth us (1 John 5:14).

And in that day ye shall ask me nothing. Verily, verily, I say unto you, whatsoever ye shall ask the Father in my name, he will give it you (John 16:23).

The law of petition is founded on the power of prayer and the Godly promises made to believers who will pray. Understanding these simple rules for prayer will equip and empower believers for maximized living. There is no substitute for a commitment to a time of daily prayer and spiritual devotion.

5. THE LAW OF PATTERN

The law of pattern mandates that when we follow a proven plan of action or model the traits of other successful people out of a pure heart, we will eventually get similar results. "That ye be not slothful, but followers of them who through faith and patience inherit the promises" (Hebrews 6:12). If you work according to a proven pattern, you will achieve the same results others have attained. It is the order of God to teach and train us by example, so when you have an ex-

ample and you do what others did, you will achieve what they achieve. The Law of Pattern was my reason for speaking boldly at the start of my ministry about the size church I would build and the size ministry I would have. I followed a proven pattern. My father in the faith and others had already paved the way, and I follow those who, through faith and patience, inherit the promise.

6. THE LAW OF PROFESSION

This law is commonly referred to in secular success circles as *affirmation*. The New Testament uses the word *profession* in Hebrews 10:23: "Let us hold fast the profession of our faith without wavering; (for he is faithful that promised)."

The law of profession is about the words you speak. These statements—spoken in agreement with the Word of God—are what the Bible promises or declares to be a profession. There are so many scriptural passages referencing this truth that listing them all would be impossible. However, here are two for your consideration:

Death and life are in the power of the tongue: and they that love it shall eat the fruit thereof (Proverbs 18:21).

For verily I say unto you, that whosoever shall say unto this mountain, be thou removed, and be thou cast into the sea; and shall not doubt in his heart, but shall believe that those things which he saith shall come to pass; he shall have whatsoever he saith (Mark 11:23).

With faith-filled words, we are able to bring divine intervention into earth's affairs. Respecting this law is critical in order to bring change into your life and to activate the power of faith.

7. THE LAW OF PROGRESSION

The law of progression says the consistent effort of a proven plan of action will eventually produce the desired results on a gradual basis! The law of progression says things change little by little—as Mark says, first the blade, then the ear, and after that the full corn in the ear. Accepting this truth will keep you from being victimized by get-rich-quick schemes. Our journey of success was not one giant leap, but a step-by-step process. Since you are going to be somewhere next year, you might as well be somewhere closer to your goals. The law of progression says things happen little-by-little, but they happen.

> *Wealth [not earned but] won in haste or unjustly or from the production of things for vain or detrimental use [such riches] will dwindle away, but he who gathers little by little will increase [his riches] (Proverbs 13:11 AMP).*

> *And he said, "So is the kingdom of God, as if a man should cast seed into the ground. and should sleep, and rise night and day, and the seed should spring and grow up, he knoweth not how. For the earth bringeth forth fruit of herself; first the blade, then the ear, after that the full corn in the ear" (Mark 4:26-28).*

KEY STATEMENT: Kingdom maximizers are not dependent on their wit to make it; they are dependent on the Lord to help them win!

We make plans based on the understanding that what limits us today will not limit us tomorrow. We make plans based on the un-

derstanding that the adversary cannot win. The Bible says we will win, so don't be bashful. Stare the enemy down.

Maximizers utilize the various spiritual laws, and they depend on the Lord to help them win! The blueprint for maximized living is comprised of proven principles that bring predictable results.

CHAPTER 4

THE BARRIERS TO MAXIMIZED LIVING

As a teacher of life-changing principles for several decades and as a pastor of one of the nation's mega-churches, I have observed people from many walks of life in countless troubling situations. Adversity does not affect every person the same way.

KEY STATEMENT: People in similar situations face similar adversities, yet respond differently.

We cannot control the destructive, devastating, and troublesome situations that come our way, but we can control our determined response in line with the Word of God! Although the maximized life can be achieved, there are specific obstacles that must be overcome which can defeat most people. The harsh reality of life, which is reflected in Scripture, is that though victory over life's troubles is promised, it is not automatic and requires purposeful sustained effort to attain.

As stated in chapter three, one of the reasons people fail in life is that they don't plan to win. Not only must you propose to win, you must also plan to win. When you develop a strategy, it is important to identify the obstacles to your success so that those obstacles can be overcome. The wisdom from the teachings of Jesus Christ is that any wise builder or leader will work to develop a strategy that identifies and eliminates the barriers to success.

For which of you, intending to build a tower, sitteth not down first, and counteth the cost, whether he have sufficient to finish it? Lest haply, after he hath laid the foundation, and is not able to finish it, all that behold it begin to mock him, saying, "This man began to build, and was not able to finish." Or what king, going to make war against another king, sitteth not down first, and consulteth whether he be able with ten thousand to meet him that cometh against him with twenty thousand? Or else, while the other is yet a great way off, he sendeth an ambassage, and desireth conditions of peace (Luke 14:28-32).

There are several components of a well-developed strategy. One component identifies the adversity and the reason it exists, and the next component identifies what must be done to overcome the adversity. In the pursuit of the maximized life, many things stand in the way of attaining your goal of a quality life. These obstacles must be addressed and eliminated so that pursuit of something better can continue without restriction.

Identification of potential danger does not glorify the danger, but it does provide an opportunity to prepare and to navigate through the danger! Signs on highways are a fine example of this concept.

I have observed sincere, well-meaning people desiring better but

who were unable to overcome the obstacles of discouragement which aborted their maximizing effort. I can remember one particular project where, if I had not overcome the obstacles, the ministry would have been severely handicapped. Our first building construction project was almost aborted. We had petitioned our bank to lend us the funds to construct a multipurpose building and, much to our surprise, our loan was declined because the bank considered our project too ambitious.

Our members had high hopes and had given their money to support the initial phases of the building project. I knew that the negative news would be a great disappointment that could slow our growth momentum. What was I to do? We were not declined due to credit; we had good credit and were good customers of the bank. Yet the bank considered our project too ambitious because we were attempting to build two buildings simultaneously, one at each of our locations in Houston. We were prepared to build one of the buildings without bank assistance, but we needed help with the second one.

I spoke to the loan officer again, a vice president, to express my displeasure and ask him to reconsider the loan proposal. A few days later he returned with the same reply; the loan was declined again. I told the banker their decision was unfair because it was based on something other than our financial strength and track record. I told him I was moving ahead with the project and, when I finished, I would punish the bank. You may ask how a person punishes a lending institution. It is done by taking all of one's money out of the institution in cash. Because banks normally do not keep that much cash on hand, it could present a serious public relations problem.

Instead of bemoaning the decision, I chose to make it a rallying point for our members. When I announced that our loan request had

been denied, I challenged the members to be a part of something special by stretching to build both buildings without bank assistance.

The Sunday I shared this with the congregation, I made a bold statement that we would build the new worship facilities a brick a day, and if God would give us enough bricks and enough days, we would complete the project. What could have been an obstacle was used as a point of inspiration and commitment. We proceeded with the project and were about 60 percent complete when I received a call saying the bank wanted to participate in the completion of the project.

The first obstacle to overcome is the Immaturity Barrier, which is the flawed thinking that one's success is the responsibility of others. This misguided expectation normally leads to disappointment and the blame of others for one's lack of progress. To mature is to accept responsibility for one's own future. I remember when I realized that I had to take responsibility for my quality of life, and that I could only blame myself if I failed or succeeded. I chose to take decisive action to improve my life, my marriage, and my ministry. It was a liberating moment.

The second obstacle to be addressed is the Ignorance Barrier, or the lack of knowledge which seems to be present in the initial phase of any pursuit. The ancient prophet Hosea wrote that people are destroyed for a lack of knowledge. "My people are destroyed for lack of knowledge: because thou hast rejected knowledge, I will also reject thee, that thou shalt be no priest to me: seeing thou hast forgotten the law of thy God, I will also forget thy children. As they were increased, so they sinned against me: therefore will I change their glory into shame" (Hosea 4:6-7). The knowledge he is referencing is not the lack of acquired knowledge. The lack of knowledge that is tragic

is rejected knowledge, which implies a wasted opportunity. Hiding behind a lack of knowledge as an excuse for a lack of progress will not improve life, and it will not relieve one of the responsibilities to acquire the knowledge necessary to excel in life.

The third obstacle that must be dealt with is the Inferiority Barrier, which is the false belief that one is not worthy of something better. Social conditioning and stereotyping tend to leave emotional scars, causing their victims to retreat from the pursuit of personal progress. The tragedy is that there is nothing anyone can do to convince them they are worthy and deserve better. This subconscious chain on their thought life can only be broken by saturation with truth and exposure to others who were able to experience better.

The fourth obstacle which must be eradicated is the Intimidation Barrier, which is another internal barrier, when one perceives the magnitude of the problems and difficulties faced are beyond his ability and resources. Such resignation can be overcome by choosing to look deliberately at one problem at a time. You can eat an elephant if you eat it one bite at a time and don't try to swallow the whole elephant at once.

The fifth obstacle to be eliminated is the Inconsistency Barrier. This refers to the problem of insufficient resolve, whereby one cannot hold a course until the desired results are achieved. Only a resolve that is anchored in pleasing God will suffice. So many people stop short of obtaining their goals simply because they lack the resolve to take the next step, to make that next call, to go to that next interview, or to send out one more résumé. Throughout the Bible, the message of consistency is prevalent.

The sixth obstacle which must be dismantled is the Insubordination Barrier, or the lack of respect for authority. Rebellion, lack of in-

tegrity, and unrestrained pride have been the downfall of so many with amazing potential. The Bible teaches us that authority is ordained by God for the sake of order and civility. Without order, chaos emerges. I have worked with some very talented individuals whose Achilles' heel was their lack of respect for their supervisor, which soon caused upper management to fire them. What a waste! Taming this tiger is a matter of simple reasoning and consideration of determining what level of cooperation and respect would be desired of others if you were in the position of authority. It's the golden rule: do unto others as you would have them do unto you.

The seventh barrier that must be toppled is the Impatience Barrier, which is a lack of sustained intensity. Understanding that results are progressive and delays should not diminish our passion is critical in the pursuit of any goal. Patience from a biblical perspective is not a position of passive acceptance, but one of diligent engagement. Keeping one's eye on the prize and reminding oneself of the payoff help to develop the stamina needed for the journey.

This book is written to help the reader identify and overcome these barriers to success, as well as other barriers not listed. In the forthcoming chapters, life skills and techniques are shared in an effort to equip and empower the reader to overcome challenges and, eventually, experience a maximized life.

KEY STATEMENT: Positive change for the believer is always a product of human effort sustained by divine help!

"And there appeared an angel unto him from heaven, strengthening him" (Luke 22:43). It is the undeniable will of God that no

barrier, whether man-made or satanically orchestrated, should prevent us from maximizing life.

"No weapon that is formed against thee shall prosper; and every tongue that shall rise against thee in judgment thou shalt condemn. This is the heritage of the servants of the LORD, and their righteousness is of me," saith the LORD (Isaiah 54:17).

For though we walk in the flesh, we do not war after the flesh: (For the weapons of our warfare are not carnal, but mighty through God to the pulling down of strong holds;) casting down imaginations, and every high thing that exalteth itself against the knowledge of God, and bringing into captivity every thought to the obedience of Christ (2 Corinthians 10:3-5).

In order to overcome the various barriers we face, we must develop a mindset, attitude, thought process, and personal initiative to win in life. We must be willing to win and pay the price for victory.

When I think of the tenacity necessary to win in life, I am reminded of learning to ride my first bicycle. My mother had purchased it for me for $15 from the neighborhood thrift store. I did not know how to ride a bike, but I was serious about learning to do so.

I started to wobble as I attempted to gain my balance, and I fell. I quickly got up, brushed off the dirt, and gave it another try. Oops! I fell to the ground again and continued this process repeatedly until I was able to maintain my balance and make some forward progress. I was driven by the knowledge that others had learned to master riding a bike. If they could, so could I. Through the bumps and the bruises I endured that day, I was able to learn.

It is this same type of tenacious effort that is required to overcome the obstacles to experiencing success. Many people do not attempt success because they are afraid of the initial bumps and bruises experienced through the learning process. The effort that is put forth is determined by the desire to win and succeed. When you look around and see others doing what you are attempting to do, be encouraged; if it was possible for them, it is also possible for you. Hang in there! You can win!

SECTION TWO

THE MEDITATION FOR MAXIMIZING LIFE

CHAPTER 5

REALIZING YOUR POTENTIAL FOR MAXIMIZED LIVING

It is impossible to teach others how to maximize life without teaching the principles of meditation. There is an inseparable connection between meditation and success. I have coached many businessmen and pastors in these principles of success. The teaching that makes the most significant impact is the teaching on meditation. Get ready for an exciting journey that will help you understand how to release your potential. Potential is that which exists, but is not yet visible. This chapter builds the foundation for making the necessary personal changes to see our potential, access the necessary resources, and execute a strategic plan of action.

"Trust in the LORD with all thine heart; and lean not unto thine own understanding. In all thy ways acknowledge him, and he shall direct thy paths" (Proverbs 3:5). You must believe that if you make Jesus your Lord, then you can trust Him (His Word) to direct your paths. I know the previous Scripture says, ". . . in all thy ways acknowledge him, . . ." but I also want you to be balanced in your thinking. It is not necessary for God to tell you what color suit to

wear. He gives you the freedom to choose your clothes. He won't necessarily tell you what kind of car to purchase unless that car is critical to some other plan He has for you. He leaves those decisions up to you. Likewise, He won't tell you what house to live in or to buy, unless that particular house is essential for your destiny. Other than that, He says, "Go out and pick the one you can pay for." God trusts you to make some decisions. He says in Mark 11:24, " . . . what things soever ye desire . . . ," which eliminates the limits others try to impose upon you. Understand that embracing God's purpose in principle establishes direction and influences our decision making.

Many of the plans and purposes of God are revealed progressively, so we must learn to rest in the order of God. He may not tell you in advance all that you will be doing next year. God gives us information on a need-to-know basis. He will let you know just as He did for Paul in Acts 9:6.

Paul had an awesome experience on the Damascus road. He began to talk to Jesus—"And he trembling and astonished said, 'Lord, what wilt thou have me to do?' And the Lord said unto him, 'Arise, and go into the city, and it shall be told thee what thou must do.' " Why didn't God tell him when he asked the question? God wanted him to understand that He would give the answer to him piecemeal. It's the same for you and me. There are some things that God wants you to do that He knows you can't handle right now. So, you should rest in the knowledge that when you need to know, you will know.

Living the abundant life that Jesus came to give us is accomplished by releasing both our natural potential and our spiritual potential.

"I can do all things through Christ who strengthens me" (Philippians 4:13 NKJV). This Scripture means you can do all things (that are ordained of God). I want to teach you how to release this poten-

tial to do all things pertaining to your purpose and destiny through the principle of meditation.

"Now unto him that is able to do exceeding abundantly above all that we ask or think, according to the power that worketh in us, unto him be glory in the church by Christ Jesus throughout all ages, world without end. Amen" (Ephesians 3:20-21). According to this passage, the "exceeding abundantly above" will come to pass based on the power working inside of us. The Bible is full of passages, such as this one, that let us know that God has uniquely engineered us with what I call "dormant abilities." These abilities must be ignited and released. You must wake them up.

Think of your untapped potential as a seed. A seed is a powerful thing. It is programmed to be more than it presently is, and it does not look like anything that it will become. In the Bible, we get an idea of the nature of God and how He does things. "And God said, 'Let the earth bring forth grass, the herb yielding seed, and the fruit tree yielding fruit after his kind, whose seed is in itself, upon the earth:' and it was so" (Genesis 1:11). In this Scripture, God is talking about the seed inside of the fruit.

KEY STATEMENT: In order for the seed to release its created potential, it has to be introduced to an environment that wakes it up.

If it's not introduced to the right environment, it will always be in a potential state, never achieving the program that God put inside of it. Man is the same way. When I was running the streets of Houston's Fifth Ward ghetto, I had everything inside of me then to be-

come who I am right now. Although it didn't seem possible back then, all I needed was to be placed in the right environment that would release the program that God had placed inside of me.

Seeds also require outside resources to develop into what they have been designed to become. Understand that you are in seed form right now, but there are some things you need outside of yourself that are going to help you become who God wants you to be.

KEY STATEMENT: Within a seed, there is the potential for a forest.

As I mentioned earlier, potential is what exists but is not yet visible. In the case of Adam, inside of him was the entire human race. So when God looked at Adam, He didn't only see Adam, He saw everything Adam would produce. Likewise, when God looks at you, He doesn't only see you in the state you're in now, but He sees everything you can become. That's why when God talks to us, He talks to us in the future tense, as though we are already what He wants us to become.

> *And the angel of the LORD appeared unto him, and said unto him, "The LORD is with thee, thou mighty man of valour" (Judges 6:12).*

> *Blessed be the God and Father of our Lord Jesus Christ, who hath blessed us with all spiritual blessings in heavenly places in Christ (Ephesians 1:3).*

KEY STATEMENT: Releasing potential and realizing potential are matters of choice and not chance.

We can shout all day long about a program of success being engineered on the inside of you, but until you know how to release it, you will be prone to scale back your expectations. You will tend to stay within the limits others have placed on you. But God has so much more planned for you! You may have allowed others to restrict your dreams and suppress your expectations for so long that it may now be difficult for you to see beyond the limits others have placed on you. You need to know that you cannot go to the next level in life until you can internally see yourself there. Others will encourage you, but don't restrict your dreams to what others can dream for themselves. However, God may want to raise you above their dream for you. Years ago I had dreams of unconventional church ministry in multiple locations, traveling to the services via helicopter. Pastors saw no need for a helicopter and attempted to abort my dream because they could never see themselves flying in an aircraft. I refused to let their lack of vision limit me.

This story about Joshua's encounter at Jericho clearly illustrates the principle of seeing yourself with end results of what God promises. "Now Jericho was straitly shut up because of the children of Israel: none went out, and none came in. And the LORD said unto Joshua, 'See, I have given into thine hand Jericho, and the king thereof, and the mighty men of valour' " (Joshua 6:1-2). They had not done anything thus far, yet God told Joshua that He had already given it to them. God had already taught Joshua this principle, telling him, "Thou shalt meditate [on the Word] day and night, that thou mayst observe to do according to all that is written therein . . . " (Joshua 1:8). But in chapter six God sat Joshua down and told him to see himself at the next level. This is the way God operates. This principle I want to share with you is one that God taught me in the past.

Years ago, I was in a little, rundown, dilapidated church in Houston, Texas, on West Montgomery Road in a five-foot-by-five-foot closet that had been converted into a makeshift office. In this little space, God taught me how to meditate on the Word. He taught me how to release the potential that was inside of me. People who looked at my pitiful state at that time would laugh at me, but they did not know what God had deposited in me. I looked nothing like what I would become, but the program was still inside. God taught me how to tap into the reservoir of potential by showing me how to see myself at the next level of productivity. I want you to understand this point, because if you are going to release your potential and maximize your life, then you have to see yourself there before you get there. Otherwise, you will never get there. I want you to understand that there is a certain way you have been designed by God to think and dream.

KEY STATEMENT: Your thinking and imagination either liberate or
      limit you.

Some of you are limited now because you have been conditioned to envision yourself in a limited way. You have been trained to just barely survive. You have not been conditioned to dream big or expect something extraordinary to happen to you. Most people have become conditioned to look upon people who have material surplus with disdain, despising those who have acquired more than they have themselves. The reason for this kind of jealousy and envy is what I call "having a pie mentality." You think there's only so much success out there, so if someone else gets a piece of the success pie,

then there must be less available for you. You must learn to change that mindset, because you are limiting yourself based on what others have.

It was startling when I found out that in order to transform us, God works within the confines of the way we are designed to function. Our belief system has been shaped by several factors that greatly influence our behavior. These factors are our environment, the influence of authority figures, repetitive information, and life's experiences. The most potent impact on our belief system is an experience.

Every experience has three basic components: words, images, and emotions. God has uniquely designed you for several types of experiences within this broader human experience.

KEY STATEMENT: Life experiences have the most potent impact on what you believe about yourself and what you can envision for your future.

The way experiences impact your life is expressed in the following illustration. Imagine a chair that everybody sits on. The manufacturer says the chair will hold the weight of any person. People sit in the chair all day who look like they weigh more than you do, and the chair holds them. Then you come along and sit in the chair, but it crumbles under your weight. What are you going to believe about the chair? You will believe the chair cannot hold your weight. Regardless of what you have seen others do, your experience strongly influences what you believe. Consider the basic experience types:

1. *Natural experiences are those you actually live out.* These are those day-to-day encounters we have that are common to life.

The natural experiences are those events that we are involved in during the course of our lives.

2. *Soulish experiences are those that take place in your mind.* They are similar to a dream where everything seems so real. For instance, maybe someone is chasing you. Although you never leave your bed, you wake up perspiring with your heart beating rapidly. Why? Because your belief system sees those mental pictures and says, "Someone is chasing you," and when someone is chasing you, you run. Naturally when you run your heart beats fast and you perspire. This happens because on the inside this has all become real to you. Your belief system does not easily distinguish between these various experiences.

3. *Spiritual experiences are those that are initiated by God.* Whenever God wants to take a person to the next level, He may give them visions and dreams. Why does He do this? Because it is the order of God to change a man on the inside first, so that he can impact the outside world. You can't be limited by what you see others do. God can't achieve anything great on the earth if we limit ourselves. God is doing great things at New Light Church, but I don't want the other pastors in America to be limited by what they see our ministry accomplish. Your God-designed program may exceed the program of the one teaching you or the one you admire.

"I have more understanding than all my teachers: for thy testimonies are my meditation" (Psalm 119:99). Your belief system, which is influenced greatly by your experiences, cannot distinguish between these various kinds of experiences. Through meditation,

man initiates spiritual experiences that can positively affect his belief system to cause superior performance and ultimate success!

Your belief system is responsible for several success factors, such as your comfort zone management. Your comfort zone is a place where you feel at ease. If you get out of your comfort zone, your comfort zone management tells you, "You don't belong there—get back." So you begin to make decisions to bring yourself back to your comfort level. This is important to understand because if you choose to go to another level and get there before your comfort zone is acclimated, you're not going to stay there for long because the law of your mind says that you are going to shut down. You are going to believe that you're not supposed to be at that level. You will believe that you made a mistake when you moved to a certain neighborhood or bought a certain car. You may say things like "I made a mistake accepting this job because everyone who works here has a degree, but I don't." And pretty soon you are going to make choices or mistakes that will lead you back to where you were before.

You can take people out of the ghetto and put them in the suburbs, but unless there is a change in mindset, they can easily turn the suburb into a ghetto. Unless they have suburb mentalities, their comfort levels with the filth and clutter of the ghetto will gradually bring changes in the environment. In their thinking, they have a tolerance for filth, for things like broken windows and run down cars sitting in their driveway. You see, little by little, we tend to manifest the inner image we have of ourselves.

Your belief system is also responsible for your ability to recognize resources. One of the main reasons many people don't take a step toward "the better" is because they don't see it. Once something becomes important to you, you can spot things that relate to it all

around you. A perfect example occurred when my wife, Bridget, wanted a Volkswagen Beetle. Because this was important to her, she saw this type of vehicle everywhere we went. I didn't see them because they were not important to me.

KEY STATEMENT: Once you have communicated to your belief system that something is important to you, you are then able to spot the resources that God has already placed around you.

Your belief system is predetermined to be influenced by repetition, pictures, and other images, both psychological and physical. Your belief is based on your life experiences, because God has designed us to be influenced by the experience types I mentioned previously. The Scripture says in Mark 9:23, "If thou canst believe, all things are possible to him that believeth." This is the key to accomplishing compelling goals—believing that you can.

God wants you to dream bigger than you are dreaming now. He has no problem with that. God gets things done on the earth through someone. So if God wants to bless your family, He has to use someone in your family to do so. Why not you? God spoke to me that He rewards our persistent expectations. God is ready to respond to your persistent expectations, but you short circuit the process by talking yourself out of it—all because you don't see how you can pull it off. Meditation is God's plan to help you see yourself in a new way, triggering other success mechanisms within you that will cause you to achieve more and experience amazing progress.

In the next chapter, I will share with you what I have taught so

many seekers of success in the business arena and the church arena. Get ready to go to another level in your pursuit of God's best as you learn how to expand your capacity to believe and release the pre-programmed success within you.

CHAPTER 6

RELEASING YOUR POTENTIAL FOR MAXIMIZED LIVING

Meditation involves picturing yourself experiencing the promises of God on the canvas of the imagination. Meditation provides a spiritual experience that has transformative potential. "For I delight in the law of God after the inward man: But I see another law in my members, warring against the law of my mind, and bringing me into the law of sin which is in my members" (Romans 7:22-23). This passage suggests that there are specific laws that govern the mind. Our minds are designed by God to function a certain way, and our thinking is critical to what we accomplish in life. Your thinking can liberate you, allowing you to rise to another level, or it can keep you in the bondage of your present state. When I was in that little church on West Montgomery Road, God taught me how to dream. In the Book of Psalms, we are instructed by God to meditate, and meditation is more than just reading the Word of God.

KEY STATEMENT: Meditation is picturing the Word of God (the end
result) on the canvas of your imagination.

It is so important to see yourself as the Word of God sees you,
that is, with the potential inside you already manifested externally.
You must see the end result because what you see affects your life. We
have been engineered by God to function in concert with the way
we see ourselves.

"Blessed is the man that walketh not in the counsel of the ungodly, nor standeth in the way of sinners, nor sitteth in the seat of
the scornful. But his delight is in the law of the LORD; and in his law
doth he meditate day and night" (Psalm 1:1-2). What is this meditation going to do for him? Psalm 1:3 gives us the answer, "And he
shall be like a tree planted by the rivers of water, that bringeth forth
his fruit in his season; his leaf also shall not wither; and whatsoever
he doeth shall prosper." The success-maximizing program God
placed on the inside of you is going to be released when you meditate, when you begin to see your end result. I know a lot of people
are uncomfortable using imagination with meditation, but the same
Hebrew word translated "meditate" is also translated "imagine."
Psalm 38:12 records, "They also that seek after my life lay snares for
me: and they that seek my hurt speak mischievous things, and imagine deceits all the day long." So when you meditate, you are using the
canvas of your imagination to see the end result.

There is great potential inside of you, but until you start dreaming (meditating), you are not going to release it. Your comfort zone
is going to keep you right where you are until you change its coordinates. The advertising industry understands this principle. They

know that if they take an actor with whom you have associated good feelings and they get this actor to endorse their product, you will believe you are supposed to have that particular product. You then walk through the store searching for that product because you have been conditioned through the repetitious commercials to believe that it is the best product for you. Even though you compare the product with a similar product, something on the inside tells you the brand you've seen advertised day and night is the one you're supposed to have. It doesn't matter that both products are basically the same and the commercialized one costs more. Your belief system has been impacted by what you have seen over and over.

When God wanted to take a man to the next level, He always gave him a vision. Such visions were like a spiritual commercial on the canvas of his imagination that affected his belief system:

The hand of the LORD was upon me, and carried me out in the spirit of the LORD, and set me down in the midst of the valley which was full of bones, and caused me to pass by them round about: and, behold, there were very many in the open valley; and, lo, they were very dry. And he said unto me, "Son of man, can these bones live?" And I answered, "O Lord GOD, thou knowest." Again he said unto me, "Prophesy upon these bones, and say unto them, 'O ye dry bones, hear the word of the LORD. Thus saith the Lord GOD unto these bones; "Behold, I will cause breath to enter into you, and ye shall live: And I will lay sinews upon you, and will bring up flesh upon you, and cover you with skin, and put breath in you, and ye shall live; and ye shall know that I am the LORD." ' " So I prophesied as I was commanded: and as I prophesied, there was a noise, and behold a shaking, and the bones came together, bone to his bone. And when I beheld, lo,

the sinews and the flesh came up upon them, and the skin covered them above: but there was no breath in them. Then said he unto me, "Prophesy unto the wind, prophesy, son of man, and say to the wind, 'Thus saith the Lord GOD; "Come from the four winds, O breath, and breathe upon these slain, that they may live." ' " So I prophesied as he commanded me, and the breath came into them, and they lived, and stood up upon their feet, an exceeding great army. Then he said unto me, "Son of man, these bones are the whole house of Israel: behold, they say, 'Our bones are dried, and our hope is lost: we are cut off for our parts.' Therefore prophesy and say unto them, 'Thus saith the Lord GOD; "Behold, O my people, I will open your graves, and cause you to come up out of your graves, and bring you into the land of Israel. And ye shall know that I am the LORD, when I have opened your graves, O my people, and brought you up out of your graves, And shall put my spirit in you, and ye shall live, and I shall place you in your own land: then shall ye know that I the LORD have spoken it, and performed it," saith the LORD' " (Ezekiel 37:1-14).

In that Scripture, God takes Ezekiel into a valley of dry bones. He was never there physically, but on the canvas of his imagination (in the spirit) God painted this scenario. In the vision, Ezekiel saw himself walking in the valley of dry bones and preaching to the bones, watching the bones come together. Remember that your belief system cannot distinguish between a spiritual experience and a physical experience. On the inside, Ezekiel believed he was actually walking through the valley. When he awoke from the vision, God told him to go and preach a message of unity to His people. Since Ezekiel had seen himself doing it in the vision, his potential was released to go and do it in the natural world.

Another example of God using this principle occurred with Abram. When Abram doubted both himself and God's ability to bless him, he prayed, and in a vision God took him out on a starry night and told him that He would bless him with multitudes. Well, Abram had no idea what multitudes were, so God told him to look at the stars and imagine a face on every star. When Abram did that, God said, "So shall thy seed be." And the Bible says, "and he believed in the LORD" (Genesis 15:6).

KEY STATEMENT: Where there is clarity of vision, there is acceleration toward the known goal.

We need these kinds of visual boosters to help crystallize, clarify, and make more vivid the end result.

Still another example of this principle is found in Joshua. God told Joshua, "as I was with Moses, so shall I be with you." What God was doing was giving Joshua a reference point for his vision. God was telling him to see himself like Moses, and the way He operated with Moses would be the same way He would operate with Joshua.

Now after the death of Moses the servant of the LORD it came to pass, that the LORD spake unto Joshua the son of Nun, Moses' minister, saying, "Moses my servant is dead; now therefore arise, go over this Jordan, thou, and all this people, unto the land which I do give to them, even to the children of Israel. Every place that the sole of your foot shall tread upon, that have I given unto you, as I said unto Moses. From the wilderness and this Lebanon even unto the great river, the river Euphrates, all the land of the Hittites, and unto the

great sea toward the going down of the sun, shall be your coast. There shall not any man be able to stand before thee all the days of thy life: as I was with Moses, so I will be with thee: I will not fail thee, nor forsake thee" (Joshua 1:1-5).

KEY STATEMENT: You know what you know based on what you have already known.

This is not a play on words. Let me explain. Knowledge is built upon knowledge. If you had never seen a particular car and I attempted to describe the vehicle, then it would be very difficult for you to understand or identify the automobile in a parking lot. However, if you were somewhat familiar with a particular car and I described its make, model, and color, the vision of the car would become so clear to you that eventually you could walk into the parking lot and pick out the car I was describing. Knowledge is built upon knowledge.

Years ago, the Spirit of God told me to see myself preaching to thousands. I was impressed by the Spirit of God to regularly go and sit in the large 3,000-seat sanctuary of First Baptist Church in Houston, Texas, just off Interstate 10. I would imagine it full of people. (All visualizations must have a reference.) There were about three thousand chairs in the church at that time. I would imagine myself preaching to all of these people—seeing it and painting a picture on the canvas of my imagination. God taught me to see myself in a developed state. I could not explain it back then because God had not given me the scriptural validation for it. I was just obedient. I would do that several times a week. The people at the church allowed me

to go inside, thinking I went there to pray. I was doing more than just praying; I was releasing my potential. I was doing it repetitively because my belief system, like that of most people, is affected by repetition. Whenever I attempt extraordinary projects, I first see them completed on the canvas of my imagination. We can escape the discomforts of our present state by visiting our future on the canvas of our imagination.

Let's look at one more example of this principle in operation. Hebrews 6:12 tells us that we should "Be followers of them who through faith and patience inherit the promises." I am not exposing you to a strange teaching or some foreign principle. It may sound odd to you, but it is the practical will of God for us to study, to model the application of successful principles we see in the lives of successful people. So if you want to go there, you need to find someone who is already there, hang around them (if possible), or read the books written about them. Doing so will help crystallize an image of yourself in the same spot.

God taught Jacob to be successful with this principle. (See Genesis 30—31.) He gave Jacob a success plan, and He showed him how to envision its end result. He told Jacob to believe that spotted and speckled cows would be produced from solid cows. He gave him a plan of action of putting rods together in the watering troughs where the cows would come to mate and drink. Jacob peeled back the bark so that it would look like the kind of cattle hide he wanted the new calves to possess. The genetic miracle did not happen because the cows saw it, but because Jacob saw it. The Bible clearly declares that God taught Jacob this technique. If Jacob had owned a camera, he would have taken a picture and put it before him. But he didn't, so he had to improvise. We have the opportunity to take photos of the things we want so that we can imagine them clearly.

Remember, where there is clarity of vision, there is acceleration. It's like when you drive in the fog. Even though you know
where you're going, you are forced to drive slowly because there is
no clarity of vision. But when the fog lifts, you can accelerate toward your destination. By using and applying this biblical principle,
I was able to acquire our helicopter. I began getting pictures of hel-
icopters and putting them all around me. I didn't know anyone who
had a helicopter, so I couldn't follow or mark them. Instead, I had
to rely on the meditation principle to help me. I had those photos
everywhere I looked. Why? Because I had to release the program on
the inside of me. I had to paint it on the canvas of my imagination.
The more I began to do that and see myself in a helicopter, something happened. I began spotting resources all around me. After
spending several days meditating and thanking God for a helicopter, I drove by a place I had passed for years but never noticed. It
was called Helicopter Services. It had been there all along, but I
had never seen it. When you communicate to your belief system
that something is important to you, it automatically highlights
things around you that are related to what has been established as
important. Once I saw the place, I decided to go inside. There was
a helicopter there, and I asked the owner if I could sit in it. He said,
"Sure, go right ahead." Once I sat in it, I asked if I could charter it;
I needed to ride in it. I was getting closer to my goal, making an investment on the inside. I was uncomfortable at first, but I slowly
but surely was changing the coordinates of my comfort zone. After
a few days of flying, I looked over at my wife and said, "I'm there!
It's time! I can buy one now!"

Most of the time when I have a construction project, I have a
scale model of it built because it helps me to see it more clearly. I had

a model of the five-thousand-seat church we later built. This scale model wasn't built for fun. This was an investment in my imagination—it was an investment in my potential to achieve my goal. The Bible tells us to follow those who, through faith and patience, received the promises.

The Bible says God wants to give us the kingdom. Someone may ask, "Is that the only way to go?" No, it's not the only way to accomplish your goals, but it's the way God taught me to get there. When you do it, it's an investment! If you want another house, it won't cost you to dream. Go by the realtor's office and ask for a brochure. Take the brochure home and put it up where you can see it on a wall, a mirror, a bulletin board; somewhere. Then remind God of His Word, which says He gives you the desires of your heart. Remind Him that you're living a holy life and how much you love Him. Remind God of what He has promised you. If you abide in Him and His Word abides in you, then you can ask what you will. Then tell yourself that you believe that you will receive your new home or car. This prepares you. It triggers something to start happening on the inside. This is God's way of releasing potential within you. My wife and I use this process all the time. The Bible says that God wants to give you the kingdom. It's not a strain for God. Stop being satisfied with where you are! Begin the process of believing for better!

When you initiate this process, something happens. You become pregnant with your dream. Remember, the larger the animal, the longer the carrying process. It takes longer for an elephant to reproduce than it does for a mouse. If you have a big vision, you may have to let it incubate a little longer. And one sure thing about pregnancy is that you must deliver. Delivery is just a matter of time. God has put greatness within you. He has put inside of you more than what you

are right now. Unfortunately, you have let others talk you out of it, but I'm going to talk you into it. You are a King's child, and you deserve better!

You have to be bold enough to do it! I wish I could do it for you, but I can't. It's something you must do for yourself. Find a picture of what you are hoping for and place it where you are going to see it every day! Begin the process. What do you have to lose? And look at what you have to gain.

You may not be where you are going, but you're on your way. You may have dreams inside of you that others have told you are beyond your limits. I believe you can have a better house! I believe you can have a better car! I believe you can pay off all of your debts! I don't care what your education says. I believe you are the head and not the tail! I believe you are above only and not beneath! I believe you can have abundance! The Scripture says it, and I believe it! I can believe it, but ultimately the choice is yours. I can lead you to it; however, you have to reach out and grab it. As you reach out and grab it, something will change and you will no longer feel comfortable where you are. God will eventually give you a plan of action. That's the next step after you've become pregnant and incubated your idea. God will give you a strategy to use in the natural world to bring it to pass. God will arrange favor to be attracted to you. Others will help you get there. Because you are a believer and you are God's property, you have the God-factor operating for you. The statistics and stereotypes don't limit you anymore. God will help you reach your God-inspired goals.

Who would have thought the preacher who used to wear the same shiny suit over and over would someday give away one hundred suits in a year's time? Who would have imagined that the little

preacher whose church everybody predicted would only last six months would be raised to the level of national prominence? Who would have dreamed that the same preacher whose car was broken down, who had no money for repairs, and who had to drive an old school bus would one day fly in a helicopter and a private jet? Who would have guessed that the girl who had to help her husband hang sheetrock in a church they were renting would one day establish church campuses and pastor a church with an asset value exceeding $80 million? Can you understand why it's important to heed the information I share with you? The Bible says follow them who through faith and patience inherit the promise. I invite you to take the first step!

SECTION THREE

THE MENTALITY FOR MAXIMIZING LIFE

CHAPTER 7

THE FOUNDATION FOR MAXIMIZED THINKING

The quality of life you experience depends on you, and the key to unlocking your potential for achieving a quality life is learning to think like a winner! To begin, let's establish an extremely important definition: A winner is one who excels in life, fulfilling God's purposes and plans with superior effort while maximizing life's situations to the glory of God.

> And God said, "Let us make man in our image, after our likeness: and let them have dominion over the fish of the sea, and over the fowl of the air, and over the cattle, and over all the earth, and over every creeping thing that creepeth upon the earth." So God created man in his own image, in the image of God created he him: male and female created he them. And God blessed them, and God said unto them, "Be fruitful and multiply, and replenish the earth, and subdue it: and have dominion over the fish of the sea, and over the fowl of the air, and over every living thing that moveth upon the earth" (Genesis 1:26-28).

God commanded Adam to be fruitful, multiply, subdue, and dominate. God put into man everything necessary to accomplish these

commands. It is also worth noting that these are precise, decisive terms. When God spoke these words, man became all that God had spoken. The devil perverted His creation, of course, but Jesus came to restore us and put us back on track.

We have been designed by God to succeed. However, you cannot unlock your potential to become the winner that you are unless you learn how to think and maximize your tripartite (body, spirit, and soul) makeup.

"And the very God of peace sanctify you wholly, and I pray God your whole spirit and soul and body be preserved blameless unto the coming of our Lord Jesus Christ" (1 Thessalonians 5:23). Man is created tripartite—we are spirit beings who live in physical bodies that possess a soul. Our souls are made up of five components: the mind, the will, the imagination, the emotions, and the intellect.

"Beloved, I wish above all things that thou mayest prosper and be in health, even as thy soul prospereth" (3 John 2). If I analyze this truth, I see that my potential for doing well in life as a believer is relative to the development of my mind, my will, my imagination, my emotions, and my intellect. This statement may come as a startling revelation for some, because many "church folk" tend to think that things are just going to happen, just going to get better, and just going to change. However, that is totally flawed thinking.

God links our success and our winning in any arena of life to our very active participation in creating our success. There are things you must do if you are to be successful. Unfortunately, that is a fact that seems to escape many people, particularly Christians, when they're on a path for "the better." They tend to think God acts arbitrarily. Scriptures do not support such a view; therefore, such think-

ing is totally adverse to what the Word of God teaches. On the contrary, God tells us there are things we must do.

Remember:

This book of the law shall not depart out of thy mouth; but thou shalt meditate therein day and night, that thou mayest observe to do according to all that is written therein: for then thou shalt make thy way prosperous, and then thou shalt have good success (Joshua 1:8).

Jesus said unto him, "If thou canst believe, all things are possible to him that believeth" (Mark 9:23).

Blessed is the man that walketh not in the counsel of the ungodly, nor standeth in the way of sinners, nor sitteth in the seat of the scornful. But his delight is in the law of the LORD; and in his law doth he meditate day and night. And he shall be like a tree planted by the rivers of water, that bringeth forth his fruit in his season; his leaf also shall not wither; and whatsoever he doeth shall prosper (Psalm 1:1-3).

We experience God's best based on our actions of obedience. Unless I know what to do and how to do it, unless I develop the five components of my soul, and unless I develop my thinking, I am not going to release my full potential and maximize my life, no matter how much I love Jesus and no matter how holy I live. Although many people do not wish to view life that way, you cannot argue with the Word of God. The Word says that you will prosper and be in health based upon the way the five components that make your soul prosper, thrive, flourish, or develop.

God has established the principles for prosperity, success, and maximized living. One of the principles for success involves accurate

thinking and proper management of one's thought life. The value of accurate thinking in planning and implementing strategies of success cannot be overestimated.

We are now at an excellent point to look at an example of the importance that God places on accurate thinking. Let's consider Joshua who spent years being mentored by Moses. Moses was a leader for all times and a man in whose footsteps anyone would be pleased to follow. However, despite the awesome way in which God used Moses, there came a point in time when God informed Joshua, Moses' protégé, that his future was based on some things that Joshua had to do himself:

> *Only be thou strong and very courageous, that thou mayest observe to do according to all the law, which Moses my servant commanded thee: turn not from it to the right hand or to the left, that thou mayest prosper whithersoever thou goest. This book of the law shall not depart out of thy mouth; but thou shalt meditate therein day and night, that thou mayest observe to do according to all that is written therein: for then thou shalt make thy way prosperous, and then thou shalt have good success (Joshua 1:7-8).*

You see, you can't just sit around and wait for things to happen. That's not what the Scripture teaches. What God desires in principle for one, He desires for all who belong to Him. Therefore, if God told Joshua that he must meditate on the Word, then you too must meditate on the Word. He told Joshua that he had to obey the Law. Therefore, in order for you to be successful, you also must obey the Word of God. God told Joshua that through his obedience, he would prosper. In other words, you will make your most important decisions

by meditating on God's Word and acting on it. Only then will you be ready to act. As a result, you will condition yourself to think accurately so that you will make the decisions in life that will cause you to maximize every situation.

My life-changing discovery was understanding that God expected me to develop my mind. I know this sounds simple, but when you grow up in a religious environment that teaches you to lay all the responsibility for success on God, finding out later that you actually have a role to play in your success can be quite an eye-opening experience.

The teaching of the New Testament about renewing the mind is simply another directive in developing accurate thinking.

KEY STATEMENT: Renewed thinking is not a product of the new birth.

When you are born again, your spirit becomes alive to God, but neither your body nor your thinking changes. No, a renewed mind is a volitional act. There are many people who sit and listen to the Word of God, yet the teaching of the Bible does not profit them because they do not allow the principles of truth to change and transform their thinking. Understanding and embracing the mind-renewing process is critical to living the maximized life. "I beseech you therefore, brethren, by the mercies of God, that ye present your bodies a living sacrifice, holy, acceptable unto God, which is your reasonable service. And be not conformed to this world: but be ye transformed by the renewing of your mind, that ye may prove what is that good, and acceptable, and perfect, will of God" (Romans 12:1-2).

KEY STATEMENT: Renewing the mind requires training yourself to analyze, evaluate, and make decisions based on a different standard: the standard of righteous principles as outlined in God's Word.

Until you learn how to think the way God wants you to think, you will continue in your old pattern of thinking, making the same mistakes you made before you embarked on the journey toward success. You'll hope for better, but better will always elude you because the prerequisite for development is the transformation of your mental outlook.

If you want God's best and you truly want to live a maximized life, you must abandon your current way of thinking. You must be willing to accept God's standard as the guiding compass for life. God's ways and thoughts are far superior to our ways of thinking and can be learned if we put forth the effort to develop and grow.

> *Let the wicked forsake his way, and the unrighteous man his thoughts: and let him return unto the LORD, and he will have mercy upon him; and to our God, for he will abundantly pardon. "For my thoughts are not your thoughts, neither are your ways my ways," saith the LORD. "For as the heavens are higher than the earth, so are my ways higher than your ways, and my thoughts than your thoughts" (Isaiah 55: 7-9).*

Let's be clear about one thing—you don't turn your mind off simply because you love Jesus. No, your mind is a critical component in this spiritual relationship. Renewing the mind is a key step in developing a maximizing mentality.

ACCEPTING THE MIND-MANAGEMENT RESPONSIBILITY

I have often heard sincere believers pray and ask God to do something that He has instructed them to do. But when God instructs us through His Word to do something, He expects us to take full responsibility for accomplishing it.

There are specific instructions given to the believer to monitor and manage our thoughts to insure they're in compliance with God's standards. Our ability to maximize life is directly related to the degree that we learn to monitor and manage the thoughts of our mind. The Bible teaches that as a man thinks, so is he, which means our behavior is a product of our thinking. Look at this interesting text about mental-life management.

> For though we walk in the flesh, we do not war after the flesh: (For the weapons of our warfare are not carnal, but mighty through God to the pulling down of strong holds;) Casting down imaginations, and every high thing that exalteth itself against the knowledge of God, and bringing into captivity every thought to the obedience of Christ (2 Corinthians 10:3-5).

Strongholds are thought patterns (mental hindrances) that keep us locked into negative, belief-defeating behavior. It is a way of thinking that underlies all addictive behavior. Bringing your thoughts into captivity and keeping them in alignment with the Word of God is a full-time job, but the Scriptures tell us that we must do it. If you don't control your thoughts and pull down the strongholds, your life will not be purposeful. Uprooting negative core beliefs eliminates the main hindrances to the mind-renewing process.

UPROOTING CORE BELIEFS

Second Corinthians 10:3-5 reveals several things. It lets us know that renewing the mind is not just memorizing Scripture. No, renewing the mind is bringing your thoughts into obedience to the Word of God. That means that core beliefs that are contrary to the Word of God must be uprooted.

KEY STATEMENT: Thinking is a process of evaluating life's situations and information against a standard to arrive at a conclusion.

Your thinking is shaped by your core beliefs. Core beliefs are the internal standards of truth you have incorporated into your subconscious which guide your life. Core beliefs, as previously discussed, are shaped and formed by several past and present factors:

1. Your Environment—Your social and spiritual environments significantly influence what you believe about life.

2. Credible Others—People who serve as authority figures and speak into your life.

3. Repetitious Information—What you repeatedly hear influences your beliefs and values.

4. Life Experiences—Reinforcing the beliefs and values established by the other three components.

You make decisions based on what you believe is true and in your best interest.

KEY STATEMENT: The quality of the decisions you make determines
the quality of your life.

Your decisions shape your life and determine your destiny. Therefore, if your belief and value system is flawed, erroneous, or out of
line with the Word of God, your decision-making logic will be
flawed. Making decisions based on misinformation and erroneous
standards will never produce positive results. Therefore, no matter
how badly you want to make good decisions, you will end up making
bad ones. That is why learning how to think God's way and learning
how to use the tools needed for accurate thinking are paramount.

FAILING TO UPROOT CORE BELIEFS

Several things happen whenever you fail to uproot flawed core beliefs:

1. You will not release the God-given potential you have for success.

2. You will be tempted to follow the path of least resistance,
   thereby yielding the fewest results.

3. You will excuse yourself, your failures, and your unsuccessful
   search for God's best by applying some superficial, spiritual, or
   unscriptural excuse.

4. You will throw rocks of discouragement at those who try to
   succeed.

5. You will scale back your visions and expectations, thus robbing
   the earth of what God wanted to do through you.

I trust that you will agree with me that taking the time to learn how to uproot flawed core beliefs is vitally important to maximized living. I have devoted the next chapter to understanding the process of uprooting erroneous self-sabotaging beliefs that cripple our thinking and postpone possessing the maximized life. The journey continues!

UNDERSTANDING THE DEVELOPMENT OF THE HUMAN THOUGHT PROCESS

It is imperative that you understand the mind-transformation process so you will know how to change your thinking. This will affect the decisions you make and change the way you see life.

Remember, thinking occurs when you weigh information against a standard or a value system. Until you graduate from making decisions based on suspicions, assumptions, and speculations, all of your thinking will be flawed because you are not making a judgment with accurate information.

"Counsel in the heart of man is like deep water; but a man of understanding will draw it out" (Proverbs 20:5). In order for you to make full use of good counsel, you must understand the counsel given. Personal coaches or authority figures in your life may assist you in unlocking your potential, but you hold the key. When beginning this mind-transformation process, you must be aware of several things:

1. Our thinking is based on core beliefs that are rigid, but ultimately changeable.

2. Our thinking weighs information against values and beliefs to arrive at a decision.

3. Our attitude is a product of thinking, which shapes our perception and our reality.

4. Our suspicions, assumptions, and speculations short circuit accurate thinking because they rush to a conclusion without the benefit of solid information.

For as he thinketh in his heart, so is he (Proverbs 23:7).

Choosing to learn new things is critical for maximizing life! Learning involves:

1. Instruction—Explanation at the level of one's comprehension.

2. Repetition—Rehearsing the same information until a level of understanding is achieved.

3. Study—Personal focus and research to connect information.

4. Example—A sample illustration of principles at work in others.

5. Pattern—A systematic, regimented plan that consistently produces results; a plan of action.

6. Practice—Application of a principle in private to eliminate imperfections (practice is different from study).

7. Development—The acquired skill that is the product of the learning process.

No component of the learning process should be eliminated or taken lightly. Each component is critical to your successful completion of the learning experience.

UNCOVERING MENTAL HINDRANCES

To uproot flawed core beliefs so that maximized thinking can occur, you must recognize and eliminate the hindrances and pitfalls to this level of victorious thinking.

Winners refuse to be defeated. However, it is critically important that we uncover three common mental hindrances that are intended to sabotage your success.

HINDRANCE 1: CORRUPT THINKING

First Corinthians 3:1-4 tells us that even a believer can be corrupt in his thinking. Believers need to remind themselves constantly that corrupt thinking will always contradict Godly precepts found in the Scriptures.

The way we think is critical to the quality and success of our lives as Christians. It is possible to be a sincere Christian but to be locked into a system of corrupt thinking, which the Bible calls having a "carnal" mind. In fact, Romans 8:7 tells us that the carnal or natural mind is actually hostile and antagonistic toward God. By its very nature, the carnal mind goes against anything Godly. It is, therefore, crucial that we eliminate corrupt thinking.

There are five primary characteristics of corrupt thinking that believers need to assess in their lives:

1. Corrupt thinking is thoughts without the influence of Christian principles and standards.

2. Corrupt thinking is thoughts controlled by the hearsay, myths, and opinions of the uninformed.

3. Corrupt thinking is the negative, self-condemning thoughts we brought into our new Christian lives from our old lives.

4. Corrupt thinking is a reflection of flawed core beliefs.

5. Corrupt thinking is thoughts that waver and are unstable.

These characteristics of corrupt thinking cause the person controlled by them to be reactive, rather than responsive and proactive in life.

HINDRANCE 2: CONDITIONED THINKING

Every society seeks to condition all of its members to think a certain way. Although the Bible tells Christians not to be conformed to the world, even after being born again, conditioned thinking victimizes most of us.

Conditioned thinking controls the way you think and what you believe. In order to walk in God's best, a believer must break free from the mind control of this society whose thinking is often anti-God or anti-scriptural. Conditioned thinking manifests itself in:

1. Societal standards that say this is what you must be, look like, or do in order to get ahead in life. As a result, we spend our time trying to transform ourselves into what society says we should be.

2. Statistical standards that measure our lives but are, in truth, only a limit on our potentials. Statistics say people normally do this. As a result, we consciously or subconsciously say, "I can't do more than this because this is what the statistics say."

3. Stereotypical standards that cause us to believe certain things about ourselves because of the prejudiced appraisal of people from other racial, ethnic, and economic groups.

You can always tell when mental and social conditioning is at work because you will be afraid to step outside the boundaries others set for you. You won't buck the system. You need to know that such conditioning will sabotage your success in life. You won't need the devil to undermine you.

If you choose to surrender to conditioned limitations, you will surely sabotage the success you could achieve. Conditioning will keep you from taking bold steps to pursue your goals aggressively. I believe that embarrassment and shame are always matters of choice; therefore, the fear of rejection never limited me from taking bold steps. Years ago, when our church was in an infant stage and we needed a facility, my wife and I set out to find a suitable lease facility that would enhance the growth of the ministry. We found a wonderful place, but we had one problem. We had no money!

Societal conditioning would say to wait until we had the money, then go and negotiate. However, out-of-the-box thinkers are not bound by "play it safe" rules; they are daring, calculated risk takers. We sat at the negotiating table and explained the interior build-out we required. It came to about $250,000 that the landlord would have to put into the lease space. After carefully negotiating all of the costs and lease payments, the landlord explained he needed $20,000 to get the deal rolling.

We wrote a check for the $20,000 he requested. When presenting it to him, as he held on to one edge of the check, I held firmly to the other edge. I explained to him that this check was no good. I went on to give him three future dates that I thought I would be able to make the check good. I believe that, in walking by faith, I can go as far as my integrity will take me and, unless I am given favor, I can-

not take the next step. Well, the man agreed to my plan of action and leased us the facility. Our ministry experienced explosive growth.

Any conditioning that will rob you of an aggressive pursuit of your dreams, the purposes of God, or the plan of God must be abandoned.

When you become aware of any system or conditioning that is contrary to the standards and promises of God, you must fight to resist those standards with all your might. You have to fight! But, it's a fight you can win if you realize that it's an internal rather than external battle.

HINDRANCE 3: CLUTTERED THINKING

Mental clutter is the product of disorganization and being overwhelmed. Those who lack a systematic way of thinking and processing situations easily fall prey to cluttered and overwhelmed thinking. Cluttered thinking:

1. Causes an inability to focus. Your thinking becomes disjointed and disorganized because you have too many things going on inside your head.

2. Causes improper analysis of the situation. Your mind is like a file cabinet. If it is not properly organized, you will never be able to access the information you need when you need it. As a result, you will not be able to properly analyze life's situations.

3. Causes a sense of self-doubt. The average person is cluttered in his thinking because he has not learned how to organize his mental file cabinet. The inability to connect relative informa-

tion causes the person to experience considerable doubt and insecurity in his decision-making.

4. Causes "oops!" decision-making. The person who does not know how to mentally multitask will end up making numerous "oops!" decisions, which do not take into account all of the facts or costs. The "oops!" decisions often have very negative consequences associated with them.

As a teenager in my first after-school job at the neighborhood grocery store, I learned the value of organization and the need to eliminate clutter. It was my dream to become a grocery sacker because I thought those guys were so cool and always seemed to have money. My big brother was a grocery sacker, and he talked about the big tips he got from the customers. After I reached employment age, my brother put in a good word for me and I got my dream job as a grocery sacker.

There was steep competition among the sackers to be the best at bagging the groceries—doing it quickly, conserving space, and being pleasant—so that customers would request you. As a rookie, I quickly observed a mistake. Most of the guys had no system but just put items in the bag as quickly as they were passed to them by the grocery checker. Of course, that meant that most times the bags were difficult to carry and the fragile items, such as the bread and eggs, were put at risk.

I developed a system that worked and was quickly copied by several of the sackers. I lined my bags up, built a foundation in each bag with the durable items, and placed the fragile items on the top. I was fast and efficient. The customers loved it! Their bags were lighter and easier to carry; their fragile items were not damaged. I virtually

eliminated the "oops!" of broken light bulbs, smashed eggs, and crushed bread.

This simple lesson I learned years ago has carried over to other areas of my life. I take the time to organize any process, whether it is physical or mental, for maximum productivity. I have discovered that this makes life simple and easy to manage.

Overcoming Mental Hindrances

Overcoming the mental hindrances that inhibit your ability to develop winning thinking is critical to your success. You might ask, "But how do I do that?" The first way to overcome mental strongholds is through correct thinking. We live in a world where situational ethics rule. It is a culture that does not like absolutes and that does make decisions based on feelings. We live in a society and culture encumbered by myths, misinformation, and improper motives that even many Christians refuse to challenge.

We love our traditions. However, Scriptures affirm for the believer that the standards of the world must not be his standard. Instead, we are to establish a new value system. That value system is the Word of God. The Word is now my standard. To think correctly as a believer, we must be willing to judge everything by the Word.

In summation, the expanded definition of correct thinking is a thought life based on absolutes that are established by the Word of God and form the foundation for stability in life.

Sanctify them through thy truth: thy word is truth (John 17:17).

Whosoever cometh to me, and heareth my sayings, and doeth them, I will shew you to whom he is like: He is like a man which built an

house, and digged deep, and laid the foundation on a rock: and when
the flood arose, the stream beat vehemently upon that house, and
could not shake it: for it was founded upon a rock (Luke 6:47-48).

CORRECT THINKING

Correct thinking is free from the corruption of myths, misinformation, and suspect motives. It is a mental life that is based on truth and principles that can always be trusted.

The mental hindrances of corrupt, conditioned, and cluttered thinking can be overcome by a respect and appreciation for correct thinking, understanding that the value system you have is going to control your decision-making. Through correct thinking, you train yourself to have confidence that by doing things God's way, the end result will always be beneficial. "If ye be willing and obedient, ye shall eat the good of the land: But if ye refuse and rebel, ye shall be devoured with the sword: for the mouth of the LORD hath spoken it" (Isaiah 1:19-20).

CONCRETE THINKING

Concrete thinking enables one to look at the facts of a situation and not be moved by emotion or myth.

KEY STATEMENT: Facts are subject to change, but truth remains the same!

Concrete thinking means being realistic about what you see. Faith does not put you in denial. Being in faith does not mean ignor-

ing what you see in the natural world. Rather, faith allows you to deal with what you see in your natural circumstances from a spiritual vantage point.

One of our best examples of a concrete thinker is Abraham:

Who against hope believed in hope, that he might become the father of many nations, according to that which was spoken, so shall thy seed be. And being not weak in faith, he considered not his own body now dead, when he was about an hundred years old, neither yet the deadness of Sarah's womb: He staggered not at the promise of God through unbelief; but was strong in faith, giving glory to God (Romans 4:18-20).

Abraham was not in denial of what was going on in his body. He knew perfectly well that neither of them had any sexual life at the time. Concrete thinking, on the other hand, makes a realistic profile of the natural world so that faith can be targeted to change it.

You need to know what is real and what is imaginary. Concrete thinkers can go to the doctor but not panic or throw away their faith and confession when a negative report comes back. Instead, concrete thinkers target their faith—"Now God, I know what to pray. What the doctor said is a fact, but it's not the truth. Your Word is truth. Therefore, by Your stripes I am healed."

Concrete thinkers also reject suspicions, rumors, or abstracts. They deal with things that are real—the facts. They are not moved by what they see, but they are clear about what they see in the natural world. You need to know the natural facts because you can only function based on what your faith has manifested. For example, if your faith has not manifested the financial resources in your bank ac-

count, you need to stop writing checks until your faith and actions have produced the money to be deposited. When you stop writing checks you are not out of faith. You are only waiting on the manifestation of more resources to spend. Nonetheless, it is imperative that you keep up with the facts of the natural world.

In sum, as a concrete thinker you are willing to look at the facts, examine things, and do the research. You are not intimidated by the facts. Instead, you seek to know the facts because they help target your faith.

It was through concrete thinking, examining the facts, that our ministry was able to develop a spiritually-based addiction recovery ministry called Life Change Institute. During our first ten years of operation, we have seen over eight thousand men and women pass through our free ninety-day residence program with amazing success. Our success rates—in the upper 80 percent range—are astounding. We are often asked why our program is so successful. It is a comprehensive spiritual program that addresses the spiritual needs of the candidate as well as the soul's needs.

In the early days of the development of our spiritual program, we examined the facts about drug addiction and discovered that there was more to the physical addiction than meets the eye. Although the Scripture does reveal a spiritual oppression that is present in most addiction situations, there is also a psychological component which must be addressed from a biblical standpoint. Our program goes the extra step to address not only the person's spiritual need for salvation and deliverance, but also the psychological need for renewing the mind.

"Beloved, I wish above all things that thou mayest prosper and be in health, even as thy soul prospereth" (3 John 2). This Scripture was

referenced in a previous chapter; however, it is good to mention it here to substantiate our approach. It speaks to prosperity and health being linked to soul prosperity. Remember, the soul of man has five components: the mind, the will, the imagination, the emotions, and the intellect. Many spiritual programs focus on the spiritual components of prayer and love to the neglect of the life skills necessary to maintain freedom from addiction. It was because we approached the development of our program by looking at the facts and addressing what we found that we have been successful where others have failed.

As a last step, you overcome mental hindrances through controlled thinking.

"Finally, brethren, whatsoever things are true, whatsoever things are honest, whatsoever things are just, whatsoever things are pure, whatsoever things are lovely, whatsoever things are of good report; if there be any virtue, and if there be any praise, think on these things" (Philippians 4:8). This verse tells us that the dominant thoughts in our heads will control our lives. Therefore, when you learn to control your thinking, you can take charge of where you are going in life.

Remember, your thinking shapes your attitude and your actions. You can rise above any situation by changing your thinking. If you discipline your thinking, you cement the new thinking processes in your life. We have been designed by God so that when we do something repeatedly, it becomes the new process. Controlled thinking:

1. Replaces the old deliberation process.

2. Monitors and controls the emotions you display in life's situations.

3. Provides the intensive focus necessary for success.

4. Avoids distractions and satanic derailment through deceptions.

By controlling the thoughts of your mind, three things happen. First, you will control your actions and activities. Second, you will keep yourself focused on activities that bring value into your life. Finally, you will not be distracted or derailed by deceptive thoughts. As you consistently practice controlled thinking, you will have a systematic way to process things. As you consistently think like a winner, you become a winner!

In a previous chapter, I talked about saturation being the key element in personal transformation. Controlled thinking is the product of a saturation regime. Some use saturation during their devotion or their time in prayer. Every sincere seeker should establish a set time and place (if possible) to spend devotional time absorbing spiritual truths. This can be done through reading, scriptural memorization, or listening to audio teachings on various subjects from a scriptural perspective.

By all means, don't take this chapter lightly. I suggest that you reread this chapter before moving on to the next one. Like Abraham, you must be fully persuaded that controlling and monitoring your thought life is essential to maximizing every state you experience.

When we develop our thinking purposefully, we can condition ourselves to think like a maximizer, making the most of every situation. We can learn to handle pressure without panic and dismay but with a thought process that quickly surveys the situation and seeks out a solution to abort a potentially disastrous outcome.

I learned this way of focused thinking under pressure years ago when I worked in corporate America. I worked for a computer service bureau where there was zero tolerance for error, but because we were humans, a very costly error was made. One of my workers deviated from the process, did not check the control numbers, and made an assumption, resulting in the customer's report going out wrong. It was not just any report; it was a report their board of directors needed for a critical meeting, and it had to be accurate and on time. We blew it!

Our process was breached, the client caught the error, there was no time to rerun the report before the meeting, and we lost the account. It was not just any account; it was a very large account. My boss, the owner of the company, was furious. Of course, I dealt severely with the employee who did not follow our procedure, but that did not satisfy the boss. He wanted more blood; he wanted my blood. A meeting was scheduled and everyone, including me, knew it was a meeting to give me the ax.

I thought about my options and decided to take a positive approach to this critical meeting. Before the meeting, I quickly researched the positive things my department had done to solidify business for the company. Armed with the facts, I went to the meeting. As I sat looking into the stern face of my boss, I started the conversation, expressing that I knew we had blown a key account and no doubt had cost the company money. I said to him, "I know you want to fire me, but let's think about it!" Then armed with the facts, I began to recap my tenure with the company. I closed the presentation by telling him that I had been a critical factor in helping him make a lot of money in the past and that I was committed to making him even more money in the future. I told him that the last thing he

really wanted to do was fire a hard-working, dedicated, loyal employee like me. It was amazing how the hostile atmosphere in the office changed. My employer broke out in a big grin and smirked, "All right, get back to work. You owe me!"

A potentially devastating situation was aborted because I did not panic. With a cool head and an understanding of the real facts of the situation, I was able to prevail.

Years later, after building a fairly successful full-time ministry, we hosted our first Church Development Strategies Conference. It was our first national conference and, of course, the staff was on pins and needles knowing the conference delegates were there to see a first-class ministry functioning with excellence, like a well-oiled machine.

It was opening night. The delegates were there from churches throughout America. Moments before the choir was to sing their opening song, it was reported that we had a terrible problem. Someone had failed to bring the choir robes from the South Location to the North Location where the meeting was being held. What a potentially embarrassing situation this could be! How could someone forget this important detail at such a critical moment? Because many of the choir members had come to the service directly from work, several of them were in their work uniforms. It would have been disastrous to send them on stage looking like a ragtag band.

As the preliminary welcome and other activities were being prolonged, I went out of the auditorium to see what was going on. There was panic throughout the choir room. Because of my trained discipline of controlled thinking, I called the choir director into my office. I calmed her down and said that the people who were there for the conference did not know that we had a problem, so if we didn't

act like there was a problem, we would be fine. I asked her to look among the singers to see if she could pull together a few singers who were somewhat color coordinated to make up a new singing group that we would call The Light Voices of Praise.

That's right! Amidst a panicked situation, I formed a new group that would debut that night! It was awesome! Fortunately, the director pulled together several strong singers, men and women who just happened to be dressed in the same color; and they were introduced instead of the choir. Praise God! Again, controlled thinking under pressure saved the day!

CHAPTER 8

THE FUNDAMENTALS OF MAXIMIZED THINKING

WINNING IS NOT A FOREIGN CONCEPT

But seek ye first the kingdom of God, and his righteousness; and all these things shall be added unto you (Matthew 6:33).

The Bible is a success book, and although some may not practice its principles, winning in life is not a foreign concept to Christians who know the Word of God.

The Bible is the infallible Word of God and the only reliable source of information and truth. Often people interject statements such as "I believe" or "I think" as though their opinions and/or experiences supersede or invalidate absolute truth. However, testimony based on experience or reasoning rather than the Word of God is by definition both unscriptural and unreliable.

The Gospel of the Bible is not an "I believe" or "I think" gospel. Jesus, the Living Word of God, said He came so that we could have life and have it more abundantly (John 10:10). His truth is not sub-

ject to your approval or validation. Jesus' words are spirit and life. In fact, His words are the only words that are fixed, finite, and forever settled. Therefore, if a person's advice contradicts what I see in God's Word, I go with the Word every time.

Tradition can thus be a serious stumbling block to truth. It was an obstacle that even Christ confronted. Some people hold opinions and experiences above truth; many hold traditional thinking above truth as well. However, it is important to understand that tradition will rob you of truth and kill the creative thinking that produces the prosperity God desires in our lives.

"And he said unto them, 'Full well ye reject the commandment of God, that ye may keep your own tradition. Making the word of God of none effect through your tradition, which ye have delivered: and many such like things do ye' " (Mark 7:9, 13). To hold to what others say, whether their counsel is scriptural or not, is to esteem man above God. That is unwise and should be avoided if you want to follow God's plan for maximizing life.

Much of traditional religious thinking suggests that it is not God's will for Christians to prosper. Many traditional beliefs support the idea that suffering, trials, and tribulations are all the believer can expect in this life. This type of fatalistic thinking will circumvent any God-given success strategy. It is ludicrous to think such thoughts because they are contrary to biblical teaching. The Bible does, in fact, teach that we will face obstacles and persecution, but it also promises that God will help us overcome them. If you choose to hold on to unscriptural thinking about suffering and failing as a way of making you feel more spiritual, God will allow you to do so, but success in life will always elude you. "For as he thinketh in his heart, so is he . . ." (Proverbs 23:7).

You must realize that winning is the hallmark of the Christian faith. Consider the following Scriptures:

Now thanks be unto God, which always causeth us to triumph in Christ, and maketh manifest the savour of his knowledge by us in every place (2 Corinthians 2:14).

Nay, in all these things we are more than conquerors through him that loved us (Romans 8:37).

For whatsoever is born of God overcometh the world: and this is the victory that overcometh the world, even our faith (1 John 5:4).

But seek ye first the kingdom of God, and his righteousness; and all these things shall be added unto you (Matthew 6:33).

Now, that sounds like victory to me! When we face challenging situations with the truth of God's Word, we overcome.

The testimony of the Scriptures is that we win. However, winning, like any noble accomplishment, requires a great deal of effort.

It is said that only 10 percent of people will do what is necessary to improve their lives, suggesting that most are content with mediocre lives. This happens because most people abdicate their responsibility, attempting to make their success someone else's responsibility.

KEY STATEMENT: The thoughts you allow to dominant your mind will always direct your destiny.

Therefore, if you believe that the government, your boss, your job, or anybody else is responsible for your prosperity, it will never come to you. The truth is that there are things you must do for yourself if you are to prosper.

It is also true, unfortunately, that most people make no plans for the future. Without positive goals, you will be influenced by negative individuals. Without affirmative goals and plans, you will simply drift from event to event. There is, however, a better way.

Since you will spend the rest of your life in your future, why not spend time planning the events you will experience? Don't be driftwood, uncontrollably riding the waves of life from one event to another. Through accurate thinking, you can plan your waves.

"But be ye doers of the word, and not hearers only, deceiving your own selves" (James 1:22). Don't stay in the same boat you're in, hoping things will get better. You can think the way God wants you to think. It's simply a matter of doing the things I am sharing with you.

MODELED FOR SUCCESS

Remember, as mentioned in a previous chapter, it is the order of God for us to model the attributes of other successful people. Hebrews 6:12 tells us that we are to follow those who, through faith and patience, inherit the promises. The word "follow" in this Scripture comes from the same root word that means "imitate." Therefore, you are to find successful people in the Word and/or successful righteous people in our generation to study and imitate. In other words, study the way other winners think and process information, and then do likewise. Mind you, we are calling for imitation, not emulation, which is competing with evil intent. The Scripture condemns emulation but instructs us to imitate godly characteristics of others. If you

don't learn to think like a maximizer (a winner), you may lose what you have.

EMBRACING CHANGE

Technology is ever increasing and exploding at an alarming rate. The cutting-edge knowledge you have today will be obsolete in two or three years.

KEY STATEMENT: Your present earning potential is based on the knowledge you currently have.

You are getting paid based on what you know. However, if you do not learn to think at another level—if knowledge is doubling but you're not—the knowledge you have will become obsolete and you will lose your present earning potential.

Don't make the mistake of thinking you're going to maintain your current earning without acquiring new knowledge. You have to learn new things just to stay current and not fall behind. Don't be lulled into thinking your present income will remain at its present level or is going to increase if you fail to develop new skills.

We have all witnessed the demise of business and industry, as most baby boomers have known it. The terms "downsizing" and "layoff" are the catchphrases of our technological and industrial society. You are sadly mistaken if you continue to think it's the company's responsibility to keep you employed because you have tenure. You have been hired to produce, but if you cannot produce because you don't have the knowledge, then you have allowed technology and

the world to pass you by. Your earning ability diminishes if your knowledge does not keep up. Perhaps you can become obsolete, even in the kingdom of God, because you're trying to win in a new generation using antiquated techniques.

Any enterprise is built by wise planning, becomes strong through common sense, and profits wonderfully by keeping abreast of the facts (Proverbs 24:3 TLB).

KEY STATEMENT: The mind must have precepts, pictures, and practice in order for it to grow, expand, and be stimulated.

Precepts are informational truths. The mind is like a muscle and truth, principles, and precepts are the barbells needed for the exercise that is critical for the mind's development.

A mental muscle, like any muscle, will atrophy if not used. Unfortunately, we live in a society, even in the church, where the level of mental atrophy is so commonplace that it almost goes unrecognized. To have strength you must make an ever-increasing demand on your muscles. For a muscle to have stamina, you must use it.

Truths are principles to live by. You need to understand principles for living that produce results, then take those principles and run them through your mind repeatedly. Remember, thinking is simply taking a situation and measuring it against a standard. In order to think properly, accurately, and at another level, you need to know what winners do in a situation similar to your own. That is why the Bible instructs us to follow and study those who through faith and patience have already achieved what we are trying to achieve. We imitate them because principles will work for anyone who will use them.

Your mind must also have pictures. Images are a vital part of this process. Pictures are mental images that are critical for forecasting and planning. God has in fact equipped us with the ability to visit our future on the canvas of our imagination. When you learn to think, you can plan, live, and see your whole day, especially situations you are going to face during that day. As you learn to think this way, you will end up responding to situations and being proactive, rather than reacting impulsively. You will be able to do that because you will have already been there—on the canvas of your imagination. Remember, the Bible is a success book, so use Scripture to paint pictures of your victory in your mind.

"This book of the law shall not depart out of thy mouth; but thou shalt meditate therein day and night, that thou mayest observe to do according to all that is written therein: for then thou shalt make thy way prosperous, and then thou shalt have good success" (Joshua 1:8). In this verse, God tells Joshua to take the Word, which is the standard, and meditate on it day and night. In the Hebrew language, the word for "meditate" is the same as "imagine." You need to meditate, to imagine, and to picture because we think in pictures and images.

KEY STATEMENT: You must know that the environment and images surrounding you impact the way you think.

All accurate visualization must have a reference. This is why God tells Joshua, "As I was with Moses, so I will be with thee" (Joshua 1:5). It is the same reason that God used the stars and the sand to help Abram get a clear understanding of himself as the father of multitudes. When you choose to meditate on your future based on what

God's Word promises, you engage in this simple, but dynamic regimen:

1. You find out what God has promised in His Word, and you have proof that at least two Scriptures validate His promise.

2. You look for an example of someone who is experiencing the promise, and then you study their life. You read their books, meet privately with them if possible, or listen to their lectures.

3. Using this person as a performance reference, you choose to see yourself on the canvas of your imagination handling situations as they would handle them.

4. You pray and ask the Holy Spirit to help you in this visualization process.

5. You praise God for the new successful image of yourself that you see on the canvas of your imagination.

"For whatsoever things were written aforetime were written for our learning, that we through patience and comfort of the Scriptures might have hope" (Romans 15:4). Proven winners provide us with certain patterns of truth by which we can live. Incorporate the following seven characteristics of proven winners into your life along with your imaging process.

SEVEN CHARACTERISTICS OF PROVEN WINNERS

1. Vision—Winners are visionaries. They possess the ability to see the future, the big picture.

2. Realism—Winners are realistic. They honestly evaluate themselves and others, and they accurately assess the resources available to them. They are able to look at the facts.

3. Courage—Winners are courageous. They possess the inner strength to initiate action and take bold steps without guarantees.

4. Responsibility—Winners are responsible. They accept the fact that they are where they are because of their choices; they believe that only their decisions and choices can improve things.

5. Learning—Winners are learners. They are committed to acquiring the knowledge required to succeed. They understand the three levels of education:
   Current Education—Information I need just to stay current.
   Challenging Education—Learning new things I have never done before.
   Corrective Education—Correcting things I learned incorrectly the first time.
   Winners respect all three levels. Most winners also learn to multitask, because multiple tasks provide the challenge they need to stay on the cutting edge.

6. Thinker—Winners are thinkers. They possess the ability to gather and analyze information efficiently for accurate decision making.

7. Innovator—Winners are innovative. They are highly flexible, and they change their approach to situations whenever new information dictates a change so that problems can be solved and resources can be maximized.

USING PROPER TOOLS FOR SUCCESS

One of the most important things in completing a task is the tool you use. You must possess and use the proper tools because a tool makes all the difference.

Digging a ditch is a simple task that does not require a high IQ or expertise. But the task becomes more difficult when one lacks the proper tools. If given a spoon, the task is almost impossible to accomplish. However, if given a shovel, the task can be easily accomplished. The tool makes the difference. It's not always ability; it's the tool. If you have not been given the right tools, or if you will not respect the right tools, then no matter how badly you want to accomplish a thing success is virtually impossible.

Your transformation to championship thinking starts with your preparation. One of the first things you must do to prepare yourself to think like a winner is to get rid of mental clutter. Clutter is the biggest obstacle to accurate thinking and a winning attitude. It violates the principle of organization, which simplifies, processes, and frees the mind to take on new endeavors. Using a pencil or pen, a notepad or date planner, is the most efficient way to eliminate mental clutter and organize your thinking.

Developing a written plan is the key to minimizing the potential for making mistakes. Now, isn't that a revelation? When you write things down, you don't have to depend on your memory to recall accurate information. By writing things down you can establish order and relieve your mind. Writing is a basic way to use tools, but it is the starting point for eliminating clutter and clearing your path to thinking like a winner. The practice of writing is a principle.

"And the LORD answered me, and said, 'Write the vision, and

make it plain upon tables, that he may run that readeth it' "
(Habakkuk 2:2). Having a written plan of action gives you control of
the situation. You are no longer a victim of events. A written plan
allows you to consider events and decisions beforehand. The more
you create written plans that become "to-do" lists, the more control
you have.

You cannot be creative when your mind is cluttered. Once you
learn the simple art of generating "to-do" lists, prioritizing your lists,
and developing schedules to implement your written plan, you can
move on to critical decision making and creative things.

When you instill certain processes, such as developing "to-do"
lists, you handle everything the same way, creating positive performance behavior. If you eliminate the rubbish, you can accelerate the
successful completion of any task and goal.

KEY STATEMENT: Learning to think ahead develops your crisis-
thinking abilities.

If you can think of the worst thing that could possibly happen in
a given situation, and think through the method to prevent or manage it, then you will never be intimidated by any situation. That's crisis thinking.

The simple tools I have mentioned will provide mental rest, confidence, immediate control, motivation, and the ability to see the big
picture. I invite you to use them.

CHAPTER 9

FUNCTIONING AS A MAXIMIZED THINKER

THE COMPONENTS OF MENTAL FOCUS

The way you think is critical to your success. Proper thinking enables you to answer life's situations, and championship thinking brings abundance.

To develop maximized thinking, you must establish the "compelling why." In other words, why do you wish to accomplish this goal? Second only to your need and desire to obey the Word, your "compelling why" is your most critical internal motivator. It is necessary for progress and advancement in pursuing your goal. Your compelling why keeps you focused when facing inevitable adversity. It is necessary for obtaining the truthful and accurate answers needed for successful completion of your objective. Finally, your "compelling why" helps determine the price you are willing to pay to accomplish your goal.

Once a "compelling why" is established, there are three major components of mental focus that every winner must master.

1. MAXIMIZERS ARE TRUTH CONSCIOUS

If truth (God's Word) is your standard and you will make decisions that are in agreement with what the Word of God says, then you will never be distracted by lies, misinformation, and assumptions. Doing so ensures victory.

Some years ago a television preacher launched a vicious attack against my ministry and me. He made several fabricated allegations. He knew they were untrue. At that time, this particular minister was attacking pastors and churches across denominational lines. I guess he had some personal issues he was trying to work through. Unfortunately, he attacked my character and my good name, which immediately caused me to be angry. I went to my mentor and spiritual father who spoke something to me that caused me to regain my focus. He said, "Ira, the Word of God says nothing shall by any means hurt you." Indeed, Luke 10:19 tells us, "Behold, I give unto you power to tread on serpents and scorpions, and over all the power of the enemy: and nothing shall by any means hurt you."

Now, that was the scriptural truth that I had to believe. Our ministry had invested precious television time for teaching the Word of God to the lost and hurting. I could not stoop so low as to use that time just to launch a counter-attack. God told me, "I made your name to be respected, and I will see to it that it is respected." I had to remind myself that the spiritual truth I live by states that no weapon formed against me shall prosper.

But no weapon that is formed against you shall prosper, and every tongue that shall rise against you in judgment you shall show to be in the wrong. This [peace, righteousness, security, triumph over opposi-

tion] is the heritage of the servants of the Lord [those in whom the ideal Servant of the Lord is reproduced]; this is the righteousness or the vindication which they obtain from Me [this is that which I impart to them as their justification], says the Lord (Isaiah 54:17 AMP).

To make a long story short, it was proven beyond a shadow of a doubt that the charges he made against me were fabricated and untrue. When confronted with the indisputable evidence, he chose not to respond, but stated that he had decided to move on. Unfortunately, he wasn't a big enough man to recant and apologize, but God protected my name and my character just as He said He would.

In Joshua 1:8 God tells Joshua that by obeying His Word, he will make good decisions. In turn, those good decisions will ensure success. The same principle remains true for us today.

Winners, those who live maximized lives, highly value truth because truth is the foundation upon which accurate decisions are made. Winners pull back all facades to get to the truth.

"Thy word is a lamp unto my feet, and a light unto my path" (Psalm 119:105). Simply stated, this Scripture says the foundation of truth lights my way. To make an accurate decision about external events, a maximizer does whatever it takes to get truth because he values truth above all else.

Winners respect spiritual truth, principles, rules, and proven strategies. Principles are universal laws that are key to strategic planning and will work for anyone. However, there are also natural truths, realities, and proven strategies that must also be respected because they have stood the test of time.

For example, we do not find the law of gravity in the Bible. Yet

it is real, and it is a physical law that governs the earth. The study of physics has actually proven that gravity exists, and there are certain rules associated with it.

The study of human behavior has also proven some things that must be respected. In 1906, an Italian economist, Vilfredo Pareto, developed a management principle that was later modified in the 1940s by Dr. Joseph Juran. Dr. Juran attributed the 80/20 rule to Pareto, but it was derived from a principle he called the "vital few and the trivial many." It has been proven that 20 percent of the things you do will produce 80 percent of the results you have in life. By accepting that truth, I understand that I need to consider and examine my actions because only 20 percent of the things I do are producing 80 percent of my results. Therefore, if I want to have greater results, I need to discover the 20 percent that's producing the 80 percent and "double up" on that 20 percent. If I do this, I will increase my productivity.

The Word of God is our standard. However, there are other resources by which you can obtain information that will reveal natural truth to you. To get to that factual truth, you must do your homework. In other words, you should read books, interview others, and listen to tapes and similar sources of information.

2. MAXIMIZERS ARE TIME CONSCIOUS

Our second component of mental focus is time. Winners respect time. Time is something that cannot be saved and reused later.

KEY STATEMENT: Time is perishable, irreplaceable, and valued. It must be efficiently and effectively managed.

"Behave yourselves wisely [living prudently and with discretion] in your relations with those of the outside world (the non-Christians) making the very most of the time and seizing (buying up) the opportunity" (Colossians 4:5 AMP). Most people tend to go through life wasting valuable time; they don't treat it with respect or regard it as a precious commodity. However, Colossians 4:5 makes a close correlation between time and money.

Winners recognize that time truly is money. They realize that they must allocate their time to activities of high value. For example, if a person makes $24,000 annually, every minute of his work day is worth twenty cents. At $48,000 annually, every minute of his work day is worth forty cents, while $72,000 annually is a sixty-cent minute. If you think accurately and properly value your time, you will realize that when others ask you for your time, they are actually asking you for a commodity with a set monetary value. Knowing this, you will be able to determine appropriately the value of the time you will invest and whether or not this is an investment truly worth making. Likewise, obtaining time commitments from others helps to keep everyone accountable for the time dedicated to a given project.

Winners also think about time economics. Your time is definitely money to your employer. Many employees, however, including Christians, act as if they don't realize the importance of time. You weren't hired by your employer to make friends and have fellowship. It is said that the average employee only works thirty-two hours a week while being paid for forty hours. That means eight hours of that employee's forty-hour week is wasted time. Using our earlier example, that's $192 weekly of our $48,000 employee's salary. When you multiply $192 by fifty-two weeks, this is $9,984 per every $48,000 salaried employee. This is nearly $10,000 of shredded money every year—wasted time and money that you can never get back.

If you are going to win, it is critical to realize that time is money. It is critical that you eliminate the time thieves in your life because those thieves are stealing a monetary commodity that cannot be replaced.

3. MAXIMIZERS ARE TACTICIANS

Tactics and strategies are the third component of mental focus. Maximizers have a deep respect for tactics. Winners understand that if they discipline themselves to develop a process and repetitiously perform that process (a proven plan of action), then God has designed the mind to subconsciously take over the operation of that process, enabling performance without much conscious thought. Developing processes and consistency activate what I call my subconscious "autopilot." Through your subconscious autopilot, your mind is free from the clutter of rethinking that process every time.

Organized consistency simplifies life and frees the mind, affording me greater thinking capacity and focus. As a result, I accomplish more in the same amount of time because I can do multiple tasks. Maximizers tend to be multitaskers. They get more done because they know how to develop processes that are performed automatically, maximizing the way God has engineered us.

To handle multiple tasks, you must have a system or process by which you do everything. If you have a process and you work the process the same way every time, then your mind is freed to do other things even as you carry out other important processes.

A COMMON SENSE APPROACH TO SUCCESSFUL PLANNING

Any enterprise is built by wise planning, becomes strong through common sense, and profits wonderfully by keeping abreast of the facts (Proverbs 24:3 TLB).

And the LORD answered me, and said, "Write the vision, and make it plain upon tables, that he may run that readeth it" (Habakkuk 2:2).

Writing is essential to developing a winning strategy and plan of action. Here are twelve vital steps that will aid you in accomplishing your goal:

1. Write the goal (the measurable objective). What is the problem? What are you attempting to achieve?

2. Establish the "compelling why" for each goal. Your compelling why is the internal motivation that will keep you on target and encourage you to keep going when nobody praises you for doing a good job.

3. Establish a reasonable timetable for the completion of the objective. An objective without a timeframe is just a dream. It becomes more of a vision and a measurable goal when a timeline is attached to it. In fact, the Bible says the vision is for an appointed time (Habakkuk 2:3). So, you must have a timeframe affixed to accomplishing your vision.

4. Research what "successful others" have done in similar situations. I know this seems obvious, but most people will not do their homework. Research can provide you with a wealth of information that simplifies the process you need to follow to reach your goal.

For example, do you know where Walt Disney got his idea and vision for Disneyland? He saw an amusement park during a visit to Denmark and was inspired by what he saw. Of course, Mr. Disney

took it to another level, but his was not an original idea. They were already doing it in Denmark.

KEY STATEMENT: You do not need an original idea in order to be
                             successful.

Somebody has already conquered what you are facing or something very similar. You simply need to do your research: read books, listen to teaching tapes, go to conferences, and interview others. Talk to other people who have successfully faced what you are facing and have been where you are going.

5. In itemized form, list the strategies and options you have discovered in your research.

6. Pray for Godly wisdom and direction as to which options or strategies you should pursue. The Bible says that which is natural is first (see 1 Corinthians 15:46). The natural precedes the spiritual. You thus have a major part to play in this journey. Your part is the natural part—your research. Once you have done the natural, God will give you a plan of action. You can be confident in this, knowing that God will direct your path when you acknowledge Him in all things.

7. After you have prayed for God's wisdom, revise your list of options based on Godly insight.

KEY STATEMENT: For every step that is critical to your destiny, God is
                             obligated to make His plan crystal clear; otherwise,
                             He cannot hold you accountable.

God doesn't want you trying to guess your way through life. He is obligated to make His will known to the believer with crystal clarity. It is my firm belief that if I had several options and any of those options were detrimental to my destiny, then God is obligated to let me know it so that I could avoid it. If, however, neither of the options were significant to my future, God would allow me to make the best choice based on wisdom and counsel.

If you pray to God for direction and He appears to remain silent on the matter, wisdom then makes the choice. You make your choice based on your skills, your ability, and your level of faith. Using this process will keep you from second-guessing yourself and second-guessing God.

8. Select the strategy that best suits your faith and your resources.

9. Take "quiet time" out to think through each step of your strategy, making changes as needed. You must take time in this planning stage to meditate. This is the time to write on the canvas of your imagination. As your imagination plays out, ideas will emerge. You will begin to see things you had not previously seen.

10. Identify the worst-case scenario. Identify negative things that could happen and consider what you can do to minimize their impact.

11. Take immediate action. Be flexible to revise your plan as needed.

12. Decide what lessons you have learned through this process that can be used in other areas of life. While working the plan, you will learn lessons that are valuable to your next endeavor because life is a learning process.

The transition to maximized thinking starts with preparation. There is no greater evidence of this principle than Luke 14:28-33:

> *For which of you, intending to build a tower, sitteth not down first, and counteth the cost, whether he have sufficient to finish it? Lest haply, after he hath laid the foundation, and is not able to finish it, all that behold it begin to mock him, Saying, This man began to build, and was not able to finish. Or what king, going to make war against another king, sitteth not down first, and consuleth whether he be able with ten thousand to meet him that cometh against him with twenty thousand? Or else, while the other is yet a great way off, he sendeth an ambassage, and desireth conditions of peace. So, likewise, whosoever he be of you that forsaketh not all that he hath, he cannot be my disciple.*

Contrary to popular belief, the meat of this passage is not Jesus teaching us to consider the cost of being His disciples. That is impossible, because there is no way for us to know the price each of us will personally pay for following Christ. No, Jesus was telling us that He knew what it would take to win the world. Jesus knew how to develop a strategy. In fact, Jesus developed an awesome, earth-shattering, world changing strategy that will never be repeated!

Although often overlooked, a careful study of Jesus' ministry reveals that Jesus had an incredible marketing strategy. The basic belief of most people, even Christians, seems to be that Jesus just sort of struck out from home, preaching without having any idea of where He planned to go. But that is hardly the case. Jesus had a strategic plan.

The Bible says that Jesus gave His disciples power to do the things He did. Then He would send them ahead of Him to the places

where He planned to go. The disciples went into towns and villages healing people, telling them about Jesus, and announcing that He was on His way. The disciples advertised the things that Jesus had done and multitudes came. They strategically marketed God's best resource—the Messiah.

If you are going to be a winner, you must learn the principles of strategizing. You must learn how to develop a strategy for your situation.

There are ten attributes or components that are consistent with winning strategies that you should incorporate into your thinking:

1. Obedience—Always honor God in everything you do. Your strategy must be based on righteous principles. Righteousness must be your foundation.

2. Objectivity—You must have clearly defined goals. The double-minded person is unstable and, therefore, cannot expect to receive anything from the Lord (James 1:6-8).

3. Optimism—You must have a positive hope and a conviction that you will succeed. Faith only gives birth to expectation. Expand your expectations and give faith more to work with.

4. Organization—To eliminate the clutter that could impede your success, you must take the time to arrange your thought processes in an orderly fashion.

5. Obstacles—These expected and unexpected interruptions in your plan are a part of the successful strategizing process. However, they need not derail your progress and limit your success. Obstacles can be overcome by consistently working effective processes.

6. Offense—No battle is ever won by the defense. To the contrary, the Bible tells us that believers are to be the offense. When most Christians hear that the Bible says the gates of hell will not prevail against us, they usually believe the church is in a defensive mode. Most of the body of Christ believes hell is advancing against the church, but ultimately is unable to knock us down. However, it's just the opposite. The truth is that it is the church attacking the gates. Hell's defenses are not able to stop us. The church is on the attack. We are the offense.

   Of course, the devil would rather you be the defense, just warding him off. But let me stir you up just a little—it's time for you to attack! It is imperative that you have a purposeful attack strategy to eliminate the obstacles that would hinder you from obtaining your goals. It is time to attack everything that is keeping you from God's best. We are offensive-minded. We are on the attack!

7. Observations—In developing a winning strategy, you must become aware of resources and opportunities that appear along the way.

KEY STATEMENT: Experience has shown me that God gives you more as you follow the path of obedience than He does before you start.

Of course, we would rather it be different. We would rather understand the whole journey and then get started; but God does not operate that way. God's way is ". . . as they went . . ." (Luke 17:14). You must start, and along the way you will

become aware of resources that God has set in place for you. You become aware of things that you did not and could not see before. Winners understand this. Therefore, winners are not afraid to step forward with no guarantees.

8. Others—You must understand that other people will play a part in making things happen for you. Therefore, trust God to raise up others on your behalf and recognize the increase in productivity when there is team effort.

9. Oversight—If a process is to be successful, it is imperative that you consistently monitor it. Just because you did something a particular way before does not mean that you should not alter the process the next time around. The process may need to be fine-tuned. Oversight is crucial.

10. Obtaining—The end result of the process is not just to work the process. No, the end result of the process is to obtain! We must accomplish our objective. Winners obtain the prize!

THE WINNER'S CIRCLE

In life, there is an exclusive arena I call "The Winner's Circle." Philosophically speaking, it is an intangible, prestigious society where people who consistently achieve results gain the respect of others.

There are several ways to get into the winner's circle, but there is only one way to get there and stay there. You can get to the winner's circle in life through legislation, meaning that you were placed into a particular position that other winners worked to attain. Getting into the winner's circle through legislation is beyond your control, but it is based on the selection by authoritative favor.

For example, you've been promoted to lead a department that is already successful. People respect you, of course, because you've been promoted into the position. However, that respect will be short-lived if you do not perform.

Another way to get into the winner's circle is through association. You can gain clout and respect based on the company of people you are associated with. The college you attended and your education may open a particular door for you. Perhaps your heritage, family, friends, or the people you know give you a special advantage. Maybe the corporation you work for has a great name, one to which people respond favorably. Your association gives you credibility. However, as with respect based on legislation, respect based on association is dependent on others and will, likewise, be fleeting unless you perform.

So how do you get into the winner's circle and stay there?

Respect based on demonstration is the winning way. It is demonstration after preparation that escorts you to the winner's circle and helps you to remain. Why? Because you've earned it. If you want to win in your environment or workplace, attitude is the key!

The bottom line is that you were hired to do a job. You were hired to produce. To win in your workplace, you must decide to be a productive person. That is biblical principle.

Winners who have gained the respect of others as superior performers have done so by accomplishing challenging work assignments. If you do not seek challenging work, you will always just be a part of the pack and will never be one who stands out. Your willingness to take on the difficult task and succeed puts you into the winner's circle.

KEY STATEMENT: A person who wants to stand out will ask for assignments and complete them with excellence, speed, and efficiency.

People in the winner's circle are willing to learn new skills before they are required. They research and investigate new processes, technologies, and skills that can enhance their productivity. When you consistently perform with excellence, whether you have a college degree or not, whether you have professional contacts or not will not matter because you are a producer, a winner!

MASTERING THE THREE LEVELS OF MAXIMIZED THINKING

If we are to win in life, there are three levels of maximized thinking we must master. The first of these is critical thinking.

Critical thinking is strategy-based thinking that asks the question "Why?" Critical thinking embraces several elements that are vital to its successful implementation. Critical thinking is:

1. Thinking that is detached from the emotions and impulses of the moment.

2. Thinking that wants to understand what is behind "pushing the ON button."

3. Thinking that never assumes or speculates, but deals with the facts.

4. Thinking that respects process and order.

5. Thinking that exercises crisis anticipation, minimizing a bad outcome with damage-control planning.

6. Thinking that solves problems and implements preventative measures.

7. Thinking that sees opportunity when others see only obstacles.

8. Thinking that understands the negotiation process strives to get "the better" for less.

The second level of maximized thinking that must be mastered is creative thinking. Created in His image and likeness, we were created by God with creative minds.

I wisdom dwell with prudence, and find out knowledge of witty inventions (Proverbs 8:12).

And the LORD said, "Behold, the people is one, and they have all one language; and this they begin to do: and now nothing will be restrained from them, which they have imagined to do" (Genesis 11:6).

God expects man to use his creative mind to improve his quality of life, to solve problems, and to develop innovative strategies for the future.

Creative thinking is:

1. Thinking that asks "What if?" and answers "Why not?"

2. Thinking that understands the power of studying other creative people. It creates a library, a collection of proven thoughts and patterns (organized by life situations), and uses these resources to stimulate creative abilities.

3. Thinking that dreams as others throw rocks. It is thinking that builds roads for others to follow.

4. Thinking that understands the relationship between principles and concepts. Principles are based on a law, concepts, and practical application of that law that may vary from case to case.

5. Thinking that dreams, meditates, and imagines.

6 Thinking that sees no limits and is willing to attempt what has not been tried.

It is time that the body of Christ fully embraced the creative force God created for us in our minds. It is time that we capture creative ideas and think creatively with the heart of God and the mind of Christ.

Our third and final level of maximized thinking is courageous thinking.

"But be ye doers of the word, and not hearers only, deceiving your own selves" (James 1:22). If you are to succeed, then you must choose to do more than read and study success principles. You must take action!

Become passionate about your dream and pursue it with diligence! Passion and diligence are two attributes that affect your success. They generate previously unknown boldness and courage in your spirit.

I cannot overemphasize the critical importance of courage in the pursuit of your dream. Courage is so tantamount to success that God repeatedly instructed Joshua to "Be courageous, be very courageous." Once again, what God has given to one man in principle, He desires

for all who belong to Him. You have enemies who will challenge your faith and attempt to derail your success. Courage established by the Word of God is your weapon that defeats the enemy and rewards your resolve with success.

As you might suspect, courageous thinking has its own elements. Courageous thinking is:

1. Thinking that spawns bold action and consistently obeys the Word of God.

2. Thinking that handles pressure. Courageous thinking, therefore, looks neither to the left nor to the right. Instead, it continues to press forward toward the mark of the high calling to obtain the prize.

3. Thinking that ignores persecution. A courageous thinker knows that what is not appreciated today will be applauded tomorrow. Therefore, be bold! Pursue your dream!

4. Thinking that is persistent. Courageous thinking is full of conviction and confidence in the process in which it is operating. It understands and recognizes that as you consistently obey and persistently pursue, you are closing in on the prize!

Maximizers who win are willing to get out of the huddle and run the play. Most people prefer planning to hitting the playing field and actually running the play. You must understand that you must be bold enough to make the step forward, even in the face of persecution and under pressure. You must persevere.

In my personal study and research of maximized thinking, I gathered considerable information and gained a tremendous amount of knowledge. One of the studies I undertook, in particular, was an ex-

amination of ancient warfare strategies. Courageous thinkers are daring. The warriors of ancient days were among the most courageous thinkers. You had to have serious courage to go into hand-to-hand combat as they did in those days. They were fearless.

My research led me to one of the fiercest of the ancient armies ever known to man, the Mongolian army. The Mongolians were ferocious and merciless. Contrary to popular belief, they did not have a large army. However, they had a reputation for being fearless and having an incredible strategy.

When the Mongolian army attacked a fortified city, they surrounded the city and then invited their adversaries to surrender. The Mongolians would send an emissary in to give the adversary the choice of surrendering or facing death, at which point the adversary would often laugh at the small army. The Mongolians' strategy at this point was to retreat, divide their army into three detachments of soldiers, and then probe parts of the fortress until they found a weak point. Once the weak point was found, the Mongolians would launch a relentless attack against it in shifts. They would fight for twenty-four hours straight, wearing out their enemies. Even though they were relatively few in number, the Mongolian army was tenacious.

You will be absolutely amazed at what courage, persistence, and consistency will do. The Scriptures say it this way, "And let us not be weary in well doing: for in due season we shall reap, if we faint not" (Galatians 6:9). Thinking like a maximizer is a matter of your will.

God's intent was for man to have dominion over all the works of His hand. Mankind lost God's intended inheritance when the first Adam, through sin, forfeited his rights to be God's emissary in the earth. But, glory to God, the last Adam (Jesus) came and redeemed

and restored all that had been lost. He had only one requirement—
those who would receive His inheritance must receive His Son so
that we might become sons and daughters of God. We have been
made more than conquerors through Christ Jesus!

God created you to win. I challenge you to be all that you can be
by allowing the truth of God to transform your mind into the mind
of a winner and to renew your mind with a winner's thoughts.
Choose to set a purposeful, intensive course to becoming a winner in
this life. Choose God's way. You were born to win, so maximize your
situation as much as you can! Remember, your thinking plays a big
part in your success. God designed you to win!

SECTION FOUR

THE MECHANICS FOR MAXIMIZING LIFE

CHAPTER 10

HOW TO MAXIMIZE YOUR MOUTH

One of the most important revelations needed in the Christian world is understanding the impact of the mouth. Even though the Scriptures clearly teach that our words have value, and that spoken words create more than just a sound wave, most people do not respect the value of their words. In this brief chapter I want to highlight the importance of our words and show you how to maximize the words of your mouth as a component of your spiritual success strategy.

When listening to many of the self-help motivational speakers, some of whom are not Christian, you will hear them teach about the power of words and the importance of making positive affirmations. It amazes me that so many outside the family of faith understand a principle that is laced throughout the Bible. It amazes me even more that so many Christians are ignorant of it. Often, when the factions outside the church teach a principle that works, the church world avoids the teaching even if that principle is rooted in scriptural truths. In this chapter we will rectify this problem and examine how to maximize our mouths.

We have established throughout the book that God wants us to

win in life, but our victory is predicated by how we apply the principle of success revealed in the Scriptures. One powerful principle has to do with how the words we speak affect our quality of life. There are several terms used in Scripture to refer to the spoken word, including the mouth, the tongue, the lips, and words. The psalmist writes in Psalm 19:14 about the acceptability of his words, implying that not all speech is acceptable.

KEY STATEMENT: Our words are only acceptable when they conform to God's order for correct and accurate speech.

In order to live a maximized life you must quickly learn the important principle of maximizing your mouth. Most people are highly developed in what I call "victim vocabulary" and negative talk, but they don't realize that their negative speech becomes a self-fulfilling prophecy. The Scriptures clearly teach that the words we speak really do matter. Our words are spiritual containers that impact both the natural realm and the spiritual realm.

"It is the spirit that quickeneth; the flesh profiteth nothing: the words that I speak unto you, they are spirit, and they are life" (John 6:63). This passage explains the true power of words; they are spiritual entities that affect life. Jesus came to serve as our example, to show man how to live the God-ordained life. He divested himself of His deity to live as a man and show mankind what was possible when a life is committed to the kingdom of God principles. Consider this passage: "Death and life are in the power of the tongue: and they that love it shall eat the fruit thereof." (Proverbs 18:21). Death or life in my situation is determined by the words I speak. Even though I grew

up in a religious environment and went to church every Sunday, it was not until I had reached manhood that I was told about the value of my words. Once I learned this principle, I began to study the Scripture further to find out how to maximize the words of my mouth so that I would set into motion life and not death. In this chapter you will get the benefit of my time of study as I encapsulate this ancient but profound truth.

"For verily I say unto you, that whosoever shall say unto this mountain, 'be thou removed, and be thou cast into the sea;' and shall not doubt in his heart, but shall believe that those things which he saith shall come to pass; he shall have whatsoever he saith" (Mark 11:23). This passage comes directly from the teaching of Jesus during His earthly ministry. What He says cannot be misunderstood; even when a child reads this he or she will conclude that words become the reality of life. Jesus says that we will come into possession of what we believe and speak continually.

We begin to maximize our mouths when we take control of our words and speak in agreement with the plan of God. Romans 10:10 declares "For with the heart man believeth unto righteousness; and with the mouth confession is made unto salvation." The word "confession" is a Greek word that means "saying in agreement with God." So, you and I will begin to maximize the purpose of our mouths when we learn how to speak in agreement with the way God says we should use our mouths.

One of the most effective uses of the words of our mouth is taught in Hebrews 10:23: "Let us hold fast the profession of our faith without wavering; (for he is faithful that promised)." The term "profession" is a kindred term to "confession," which we mentioned in Romans 10:10, and carries the same meaning. Speaking faith-filled

words is the best use of our mouths, and it will aid us in maximizing our state in life. The Bible teaches that faith comes by hearing, but it also instructs us through multiple examples that faith is released by the words of the mouth. Time and time again Jesus would speak words of faith that would cause something positive to happen on the earth. Jesus teaches that every man has the same ability to speak faith-filled words as He could in the faith teaching recorded in Mark 11.

It is not bondage to have a disciplined mouth, knowing that the words I speak actually work for my good or for my detriment.

KEY STATEMENT: My words set into motion things in the spirit realm
                that will eventually affect my life.

The Scripture teaches that the angels move into action when a faith-filled man speaks faith-filled words:

And, behold, an hand touched me, which set me upon my knees and upon the palms of my hands. And he said unto me, "O Daniel, a man greatly beloved, understand the words that I speak unto thee, and stand upright: for unto thee am I now sent." And when he had spoken this word unto me, I stood trembling. Then said he unto me, "Fear not, Daniel: for from the first day that thou didst set thine heart to understand, and to chasten thyself before thy God, thy words were heard, and I am come for thy words" (Daniel 10:10-12).

Further, the Scripture notes that evil spirits become subject to us when we speak faith-filled words, releasing the spiritual authority that has been delegated to us.

And the seventy returned again with joy, saying, "Lord, even the devils are subject unto us through thy name" (Luke 10:17).

Then was Jesus led up of the Spirit into the wilderness to be tempted of the devil. And when he had fasted forty days and forty nights, he was afterward an hungred. And when the tempter came to him, he said, "If thou be the Son of God, command that these stones be made bread." But he answered and said, "It is written, Man shall not live by bread alone, but by every word that proceedeth out of the mouth of God" (Matthew 4:1-4).

This is by no means an exhaustive explanation of all that "words of the mouth" set into motion on the earth. It is abundantly clear, however, that faith-filled words are critical for maximizing situations. What sets faith-filled words apart from other words? Now that's a good question. It is a question that I asked some years ago when I was in search of a better life. I began to study the scriptural teaching on biblical faith and discovered several characteristics of faith-filled confessions.

1. A faith-filled confession is always in the present tense. It never suggests a future state, but it speaks in the present as though the future has already come to pass. For example, the Bible teaches in Ephesians 1:3 that God "hath blessed us with all spiritual blessings in heavenly places in Christ." The faith confession would be stated, "I am blessed."

2. A faith-filled confession is always in first person.

3. A faith-filled confession is always in agreement with the Word of God.

Finally, using one's mouth for spiritual activities that glorify God always works to maximize our lives. We glorify God when we please Him with our lives and bring attention to Him. Praying to God is a way to maximize life by maximizing our mouths. Praising God is another way to maximize life by maximizing our mouths. I studied and discovered twelve advantageous uses of our words:

1. Our words bring satisfaction. "A man shall be satisfied with good by the fruit of his mouth: and the recompense of a man's hands shall be rendered unto him" (Proverbs 12:14).

2. Our words bring prosperity. "The lips of the righteous feed many: but fools die for want of wisdom" (Proverbs 10:21).

3. Our words have an impact on others. "A man's belly shall be satisfied with the fruit of his mouth; and with the increase of his lips shall he be filled" (Proverbs 18:20).

4. Our words can bring us health. "There is that speaketh like the piercings of a sword: but the tongue of the wise is health" (Proverbs 12:18).

5. Our words can be used to lift others. "Heaviness in the heart of man maketh it stoop: but a good word maketh it glad" (Proverbs 12:25).

6. Our words can bring peace in times of conflict. "A soft answer turneth away wrath: but grievous words stir up anger" (Proverbs 15:1).

7. Through our words we can teach others. "The mouth of the just bringeth forth wisdom: but the froward tongue shall be cut out" (Proverbs 10:31).

8. Our words can inspire hope in the hopeless. "A wholesome tongue is a tree of life: but perverseness therein is a breach in the spirit" (Proverbs 15:4).

9. Our words can bring joy into many situations. "A scorner loveth not one that reproveth him: neither will he go unto the wise" (Proverbs 15:12).

10. Our words can influence decision-makers. "He that loveth pureness of heart, for the grace of his lips the king shall be his friend" (Proverbs 22:11).

11. Our words can make us desirable. "You are fairer than the sons of men; Grace is poured upon Your lips; Therefore God has blessed You forever" (Psalm 45:2).

12. Our words are the key to our quality of life. "A fool hath no delight in understanding, but that his heart may discover it-self" (Proverbs 18:2).

God taught a powerful principle to Abram about maximizing his mouth. God had made a promise to bless Abram with a son at a time when Abram was old and his wife was far beyond her child-bearing years. Of course, after waiting a long time for God to fulfill the prom-ise, Abram grew weary and began to complain to God. Abram did not understand that for the promise to come to pass it would require his faith to produce the results. Abram understood the power of be-lieving, but that was only one side of the faith coin. The other side of the faith coin involved speaking faith-filled words.

God changed Abram's name, which caused him to speak faith-filled words throughout his life. That's right, every time someone said

his new name, he heard them say he was the father of nations. God instructed him in this principle, which activated a miracle in his body and his wife's body. After almost twenty-four years of waiting, once he maximized his mouth through speaking words of faith, the miracle child was born in less than a year.

Key Statement: Developing the discipline to make daily confessions based on God's Word anchors your faith and activates your expectation.

Here are several faith confessions that will set you on a path of maximizing your mouth:

Faith Confession for Peace

Father, I thank You that I can commit every anxiety, every worry, and every care to You. I receive from You the peace of God, which rules my heart and my mind. My heart and my mind are fixed on You, Father, and I have perfect peace. Nothing shall offend me. My sleep shall be sweet, and I shall have peace and safety. Father, when I lie down, I receive blessings from You, and I choose to cast every anxious thought on You and I know that You care for me. In Jesus' name, Amen.

Faith Confession for Overcoming Sickness, Disease, Fear, and Mental Depression

Father, in the name of Jesus, I thank You that Jesus has borne my sickness and infirmities in His own body and with His stripes I am

healed. Sickness and disease have no place in my life. I am redeemed from the curse of the law. Jesus Christ is the same yesterday, today, and forever, and I believe that just as He healed people yesterday, I am healed today. Every muscle, every cell, and every organ in my body functions as they were designed to function. Father, I declare that I will live and not die and declare the works of the Lord. In Jesus' name, Amen.

FAITH CONFESSION FOR PROSPERITY

Father, in Jesus' Name, I confess Your Word over my finances this day. I have given the tithes of my increase, and I claim the "windows of heaven" blessing for my life (see Malachi 3:10). My mind is alert, and I hear Your voice and the voice of the stranger I will not follow. I perceive new doors of opportunity opening for my family and me.

I will always have all sufficiency in all things, and You are raising up others to use their power, ability, and influence to help me. I expect daily for the Holy Spirit to speak to men and women concerning giving to me.

Therefore, those whom the Spirit of God designates are free to obey and give to me good measure, pressed down, shaken together, and running over. I believe every need is met with heaven's best. You promised to supply all my needs according to Your riches in glory by Christ Jesus. I live in the best, I wear the best, I eat the best, I travel in the best, and I go first class in life. Father, I thank You that You give me and my family richly all things to enjoy.

Satan, I bind your activity in my life. I loose the angels and ministering spirits to minister for me and to bring the necessary finances for me and my family. In Jesus' name, Amen.

FAITH CONFESSION FOR EMPLOYMENT/PROMOTION

Father, in Jesus' Name, Your Word says promotions don't come from the east, west, north, or south, but You are the judge who puts down one and picks up another. I believe that, according to Your Word, You are elevating me to a higher level of living. You are causing my name, my application, and my résumé to rise to the top so that those with authority over my promotion will call me. I have the wisdom of God in the interview process, and You have given me a mouth and a tongue that the enemy cannot gainsay or resist.

Father, I thank You for the creativity and wisdom necessary to fulfill my new assignment. You are raising up someone, somewhere to use his or her power, ability, and influence to help me. This promotion is causing me to prosper, so I have more to give to the kingdom of God. Father, I live in daily expectation of You opening doors of opportunity for me. In Jesus' name, Amen.

When I think about the commitment the maximizer must make to the principles of confession, I am reminded of this passage of Scripture: "So let us seize and hold fast and retain without wavering the hope we cherish and confess and our acknowledgement of it, for He Who promised is reliable (sure) and faithful to His word." (Hebrews 10:23 AMP).

There is no substitute for an unwavering commitment in this principle, even when it looks like it may not be working. The Scripture validates the spiritual process that triggers spiritual activity to bring changes in life's situations. It is with this understanding that there must be a steadfast, unwavering commitment which endures under pressure.

Our parents had lost a brother to a tragic industrial accident, so

they would often visit his grave to place flowers on it and to see that the gravesite was properly maintained. My cousins and I enjoyed the trips to the graveyard not because we were interested in seeing our uncle's grave but because in the graveyard there was an old hand pump. We loved to play with the pump. When we arrived at the graveyard, we ran to get to the pump because the first one there gained the right to work the pump.

There was always a little can of water at the base of the pump that was used to prime the pump. We knew the process; we poured priming water in the mouth of the pump, and then we began the pumping process! Up and down! Up and down! Up and down! It was a tedious process that quickly wore out our young arms, but we dared not stop because experience had taught us that, if we stopped the process before water flowed, we would have to start all over again. We knew that as the pressure began to build the pumping process would get more difficult, but it was also working to produce the water. The commitment to the process yielded the positive result of cool, refreshing water. Once the water began to flow, the pumping process became easier; it took only a little effort to keep the water flowing.

Now you might ask what lesson should be learned from children playing with a graveyard pump. It is the lesson that perseverance and continuing to practice a proven process always pays off. Confession is a proven principle that yields results. It worked in creation, it worked for Jesus, and it will work for you!

CHAPTER 11

HOW TO MAXIMIZE YOUR MISTAKES

This chapter will probably be worth the cost of the entire book, because most people make mistakes but have no idea how to recover and go on. As a result of not knowing how to recover and maximize a mistake, they walk around feeling condemned and depressed. Since we know about all the mistakes we have made, and we have heard that we will be penalized and punished for them, we are prone to expect the worst.

Our new birth status does not exempt us from making mistakes and errors in judgment.

KEY STATEMENT: The road to mastery passes through the valley of mistakes, but we must remember never to stay in the valley.

Maximizers are individuals who possess the strength of character that enables them to rebound from their mistakes to keep believing, keep planning, keep thinking, and keep working to experience their

full potential. So many heroes of faith have had to overcome devastating mistakes to arrive at their destiny, which demonstrates that making a mistake does not make you a mistake.

The list of those who maximized their mistakes, learned a valuable lesson, and continued to pursue their life's calling would include the following:

1. Adam and Eve made the mistake of disobeying God.

2. Abram made the mistake of lying about his wife being his sister.

3. Jacob made the mistake of stealing his brother's birthright.

4. Moses made the mistake of killing an Egyptian soldier.

5. David made the mistake of committing adultery and murder.

6. Peter made the mistake of denying his relationship to Jesus.

The list goes on and on. Perhaps the finest example is the story of the prodigal son. The prodigal son, who made the mistake of leaving his father and wasting his inheritance, eventually recognized his error, repented, and returned home.

KEY STATEMENT: Being able to recognize your mistakes is essential to any recovery process.

It is denial that compounds mistakes and aborts the maximizing process.

And he said, "A certain man had two sons: And the younger of them said to his father, 'Father, give me the portion of goods that falleth to

me.' And he divided unto them his living. And not many days after the younger son gathered all together, and took his journey into a far country, and there wasted his substance with riotous living. And when he had spent all, there arose a mighty famine in that land; and he began to be in want. And he went and joined himself to a citizen of that country; and he sent him into his fields to feed swine. And he would fain have filled his belly with the husks that the swine did eat: and no man gave unto him. And when he came to himself, he said, 'How many hired servants of my father's have bread enough and to spare, and I perish with hunger! I will arise and go to my father, and will say unto him, "Father, I have sinned against heaven, and before thee, and am no more worthy to be called thy son: make me as one of thy hired servants." ' And he arose, and came to his father. But when he was yet a great way off, his father saw him, and had compassion, and ran, and fell on his neck, and kissed him. And the son said unto him, 'Father, I have sinned against heaven, and in thy sight, and am no more worthy to be called thy son.' But the father said to his servants, 'Bring forth the best robe, and put it on him; and put a ring on his hand, and shoes on his feet: And bring hither the fatted calf, and kill it; and let us eat, and be merry: For this my son was dead, and is alive again; he was lost, and is found.' And they began to be merry" (Luke 15:11-24).

Maximizing your mistakes does not mean that you will totally escape all consequences of your misbehavior, but it does mean that you will have God's help in the recovery process. All of life is choice-driven, so you must decide that you will recover from a mistake through repentance, and then trust the repentance process for your total and complete restoration. To refuse correction because you think your cover-up plan is better than God's repentance and forgiveness is a self-deception of mammoth proportions.

If we confess our sins, he is faithful and just to forgive us our sins, and to cleanse us from all unrighteousness (1 John 1:9).

The Lord is not slack concerning his promise, as some men count slackness; but is longsuffering to us-ward, not willing that any should perish, but that all should come to repentance (2 Peter 3:9).

Since we cannot avoid mistakes in life, we must prepare the proper response to all the inevitable mistakes. We can choose to curse the mistake, which will make us bitter in life. We can choose to nurse the mistake and go through life blaming others for our mistakes. But the quality choice is to reverse the mistake by repenting, learning a valuable lesson, setting new guidelines in your life, and choosing to go on as though nothing ever happened.

When I choose to maximize a mistake, I learn a valuable lesson that helps me to never make that mistake again. Maximizing one's mistakes causes growth in character and leads to the development of integrity. The maximizing process can be summed up in ten steps:

1. Be honest with yourself, and take responsibility for the mistake.

2. Determine the full extent of the mistake and how it came to pass.

3. Repent for sinning against the God's order for your life.

4. Determine what lessons are to be learned from this situation.

5. Choose to make restitution where possible.

6. Renounce the open door to satanic encroachment in your life.

7. Choose to forgive others who have trespassed against you.

8. Believe in another opportunity to demonstrate faithfulness.

9. Trust the Word of God about forgiveness, not your feelings.

10. Choose to run a righteous course long-term.

KEY STATEMENT: When you run a righteous course long-term, God will erase the memory of your mistakes from the minds of those who knew you in your rebellious state.

You can maximize and rebound from any mistake if you choose to trust God to give you another chance. The Bible tells a powerful story of the potter making a vessel out of clay. As the potter works with the clay on the wheel, the clay becomes marred in the potter's hand, no doubt because of some imperfection in the clay. The potter does not throw away the clay but continues to work with the clay, removing the imperfection and making a suitable vessel. This story illustrates the loving forgiveness of our God, who like the potter continues to work with us when imperfections surface in our lives. God continues to work with us, giving us another chance at life's best.

Maximizers can see recovery beyond the mistake they made. Those who maximize their mistakes value a relationship with God, understanding that repentance and the favor of God is more precious than the acceptance of man. Real maximizers recover from their mistakes and lend a helping hand to others to assist them on their way.

One thing I learned very early in my pursuit for a better life was

that I would make mistakes. I have been successful in directing and overseeing the design and construction of several magnificent buildings. Many leaders have applauded my success in constructing both functional and monumental buildings, but what most people don't know is that my first building project ended in failure.

That's right. It was a miserable failure that, had I not rebounded from it, would have kept me from experiencing the success I have today. That first project was a church building that was designed but never built. It was during my fourth pastoral assignment. I had led the people to see a need for a building. We purchased the land, hired an architect, and spent a lot of money on plans; but we just couldn't get to the construction stage. One problem after another slowed the project down and drained our resources until I was forced to seek the wisdom of God on the project.

Through prayer and serious searching, I realized that the project was not something God had ordained, but was the product of my prideful flesh. I had missed God! It was not His will. It was not His timing. I had missed it! Well, what does one do to get out of a hole he has dug for himself? The very first thing to do is to stop digging! That's right, I stood up and repented before the congregation and told them that I had missed it. I asked my small congregation to forgive me of this mistake and to abandon the project. My advice was to sell the land to recoup all the money we had invested because the land had appreciated in value significantly since we had originally purchased it. All went well with the meeting and the members loved and forgave their young pastor. We eventually sold the land and recouped our money! Praise the Lord!

Of course, the memory of this failed project tried to haunt me and keep me from attempting to build again, but I understood that

just because I failed at something one time, it did not mean that failure was inevitable next time. I put the past in the past, saw it as a learning experience, and chose to move on. I approached the next building project with caution but not with fear. I was successful at the second project and now design and construction have become passions of mine! I love them!

CHAPTER 12

HOW TO MAXIMIZE YOUR MONEY

Talking about money is taboo for most people in church, because they suspect that someone is attempting to rip them off. This attitude is prevalent in the body of Christ because most Christians have so little knowledge of what the Bible says about money. Unfortunately, most Christians are not well schooled from a scriptural perspective on how to maximize their money.

KEY STATEMENT: Money maximizers are individuals who will use the plan of God to get the most from their financial resources without making excuses for financial shortfalls.

My wife are I are well qualified to address maximizing money, because we started with so little and God has blessed us with so much—we are financially independent ourselves and are a financial blessing to so many others. The turnaround in my life came when I studied the financial management principles in God's Word, chose to believe

them, and rearranged my priorities to live in concert with those principles. In this chapter I am going to share the simple principle that I rely on today in the management and stewardship of our resources.

First, you must respect that God is our maker and He has the right to establish a plan for all of our resources, including our financial resources. The good news is that God's plan is for us to prosper. When we make Jesus our Lord, we give our total allegiance to God and surrender ourselves to His plan for our lives. By the time we come into the knowledge of God's plan (spiritual), we have become comfortable with the secular (non-spiritual) order for our money.

The Scriptures establish the spiritual order and reason for our money, which establishes the attitude we should have toward money. It may surprise you to know that God wants you to succeed financially and live a life enjoying that financial abundance. The following Scriptures show clearly this is true.

The blessing of the LORD, it maketh rich, and he addeth no sorrow with it (Proverbs 10:22).

But thou shalt remember the LORD thy God: for it is he that giveth thee power to get wealth, that he may establish his covenant which he sware unto thy fathers, as it is this day (Deuteronomy 8:18).

Praise ye the LORD. Blessed is the man that feareth the LORD, that delighteth greatly in his commandments. His seed shall be mighty upon earth: the generation of the upright shall be blessed. Wealth and riches shall be in his house: and his righteousness endureth for ever (Psalm 112:1-3).

Charge them that are rich in this world, that they be not high minded, nor trust in uncertain riches, but in the living God, who giveth us richly all things to enjoy; that they do good, that they be rich in good works, ready to distribute, willing to communicate (1 Timothy 6:17-18).

Maximizing money involves adhering to a scriptural strategy for financial increase. Further, our attitudes about money must be corrected so that we can take charge of it and not allow it to take charge of us.

Many see money as a "rule," that is, money brings leverage in setting the standard of judgment. This attitude says, "Because I have the most money, I set the rules and provide a perverted sense of worth and value."

Some see money as a "mule" which gives them the right to impose their will on those who have less than they do.

Others see money as a "stool;" it becomes a source of security which we are prone to erroneously trust above all else.

Maximizers see money as a "tool;" it is simply an agent or instrument for purposeful and constructive measures. Maximizers also see money as "fuel," a resource that holds the potential of explosive increase when properly invested.

When developing a plan to maximize your money, you must respect God's order for receiving money and for the scriptural management of money. We extract the scriptural ways for properly receiving money from the following Scriptures. We are cautioned that money gained improperly will be quickly diminished. "Wealth [not earned but] won in haste or unjustly or from the production of things for vain or detrimental use [such riches] will dwindle away, but he who gathers little by little will increase [his riches]" (Proverbs 13:11 AMP).

There are four righteous channels for receiving money into our lives that must be respected:

1. Money properly received through working. "Let him that stole steal no more: but rather let him labour, working with his hands the thing which is good, that he may have to give to him that needeth" (Ephesians 4:28).

2. Money properly received through gifts. "Give, and it shall be given unto you; good measure, pressed down, and shaken together, and running over, shall men give into your bosom. For with the same measure that ye mete withal it shall be measured to you again" (Luke 6:38).

3. Money properly received through damage compensation. "If a man shall steal an ox, or a sheep, and kill it, or sell it; he shall restore five oxen for an ox, and four sheep for a sheep" (Exodus 22:1).

4. Money properly received through investments. "Thou oughtest therefore to have put my money to the exchangers, and then at my coming I should have received mine own with usury" (Matthew 25:27).

The Bible sets guidelines for the proper management of finances by establishing distribution priorities. Consider these six distribution components governing our money:

1. WE SHOULD SUPPORT THE KINGDOM OF GOD.

Bring ye all the tithes into the storehouse, that there may be meat in mine house, and prove me now herewith," saith the LORD of hosts, "if

I will not open you the windows of heaven, and pour you out a blessing, that there shall not be room enough to receive it" (Malachi 3:10).

Honour the LORD with thy substance, and with the firstfruits of all
thine increase: So shall thy barns be filled with plenty, and thy presses
shall burst out with new wine" (Proverbs 3:9-10).

But this I say, He which soweth sparingly shall reap also sparingly;
and he which soweth bountifully shall reap also bountifully. Every
man according as he purposeth in his heart, so let him give; not grudgingly, or of necessity: for God loveth a cheerful giver. And God is able
to make all grace abound toward you; that ye, always having all sufficiency in all things, may abound to every good work (2 Corinthians
9:6-8).

2. WE SHOULD PAY TAXES.

Render therefore to all their dues: tribute to whom tribute is due; custom to whom custom; fear to whom fear; honour to whom honour
(Romans 13:7).

3. WE SHOULD PAY OUR REGULAR INDEBTEDNESS.

Then she came and told the man of God. And he said, "Go, sell the
oil, and pay thy debt, and live thou and thy children of the rest" (2
Kings 4:7).

4. WE SHOULD FINANCE OUR LIVING EXPENSES AND LIFESTYLE PLEASURES.

Behold that which I have seen: it is good and comely for one to eat
and to drink, and to enjoy the good of all his labour that he taketh un-

der the sun all the days of his life, which God giveth him: for it is his portion. Every man also to whom God hath given riches and wealth, and hath given him power to eat thereof, and to take his portion, and to rejoice in his labour; this is the gift of God (Ecclesiastes 5:18-19).

5. WE SHOULD SAVE AND BUILD OUR WEALTH.

Go to the ant, thou sluggard; consider her ways, and be wise (Proverbs 6:6).

6. WE SHOULD BE SENSITIVE TO THE POOR AND GIVE GENEROUSLY TO THEM.

Let him that stole steal no more: but rather let him labour, working with his hands the thing which is good, that he may have to give to him that needeth (Ephesians 4:28).

KEY STATEMENT: Your citizenship in the kingdom of God affords you the right to enlist God's help in maximizing your money.

The most significant step in maximizing your money is the decision to honor God with your finances by supporting the things of God on the earth. When you give to churches, missions, and ministries that advance the plan of God in a generation, you are honoring God. Choose to honor the principle of tithes and offerings as seen in Malachi 3:8. In addition to giving the tenth as a tithe into your church, you should give offerings over and above the tithe.

My wife and I are faithful tithers, and we give offerings. We have

seen the increase that God promises in His Word when giving takes place. I know to some it will sound very strange and almost unbelievable that you can live better on 90 percent of your income than you can on 100 percent of your income. The difference is that God commits to bless the 90 percent you have left after you have given the tithe. This blessing will be in the form of increased opportunities, financial wisdom, concepts, and ideas. When I began to tithe, promotion and opportunities became available immediately, and I began to increase. As I learned how to release my faith for the blessings of God, I began to see more and more of what God promised would happen when I give.

I can vividly remember when I began to give tithes and offerings as a young adult. It was a crisis time in my life; I had dropped out of college and was working in a warehouse doing unskilled manual labor as a warehouse stock clerk. The company was a hardware wholesaler that supplied products to small- and medium-sized hardware stores. It was in the early 1970s and I was earning about $65 per week. Things were extremely tight, to say the least.

In a casual conversation I had with a minister one day, he said that if I began to tithe, I would begin to see God's blessings in my life. He told me that he was not a tither but that the Bible taught that tithing would bless a person with increase. It did not bother me that he had not committed to tithing; if what he had said was true, that the Bible instructs the believer to support the kingdom of God with a tithe in order to be blessed, then I was willing to do it. I began my own biblical research on tithes and offerings and discovered that what the minister had said to me was, in fact, true.

I got excited. The next Sunday I put $6.50 in the offering envelope as my tithe and gave a $5.00 offering to my pastor. I did not fully

understand how the blessings were supposed to come, but my status quo was most unacceptable and I knew I needed to do something to trigger a change. Well, it happened just as the Bible said it would. When the Bible references the windows of heaven opening up, it is talking not about money falling from the sky but about creative ideas, concepts, and favor for opportunities.

Shortly after I began to tithe, the supervisor in my department of the warehouse turned in his resignation and recommended me to replace him. I had the least seniority of all the employees in my department, but I was a tither and I believed with all my heart that tithing had made the difference and opened this door for me. Of course, with the new position there was a much needed increase in salary. I continued to tithe in faith, and God gave me an idea of how to reorganize our department for greater efficiency. Executive management heard about it and again rewarded my efforts.

I am still amazed at the favor and the opportunities that continue to come my way as a result of my commitment to this biblical principle. I am not attempting to make a bogus promise to you that tithing will work overnight to change your financial state; I am simply sharing my experience. The manifested results of working the principles of the kingdom of God are always progressive.

As I learned how to release my faith for the blessings of God, I began to see more and more of what God promised would happen when I gave. Again, consider carefully these promises that God makes to those who will give to support His causes and His people on the earth today:

> *"Bring ye all the tithes into the storehouse, that there may be meat in mine house, and prove me now herewith," saith the LORD of hosts,*

"if I will not open you the windows of heaven, and pour you out a blessing, that there shall not be room enough to receive it. And I will rebuke the devourer for your sakes, and he shall not destroy the fruits of your ground; neither shall your vine cast her fruit before the time in the field," saith the LORD of hosts. "And all nations shall call you blessed: for ye shall be a delightsome land," saith the LORD of hosts (Malachi 3:10-12).

But this I say, He which soweth sparingly shall reap also sparingly; and he which soweth bountifully shall reap also bountifully. Every man according as he purposeth in his heart, so let him give; not grudgingly, or of necessity: for God loveth a cheerful giver. And God is able to make all grace abound toward you; that ye, always having all sufficiency in all things, may abound to every good work (2 Corinthians 9:6-8).

Honour the LORD with thy substance, and with the firstfruits of all thine increase: So shall thy barns be filled with plenty, and thy presses shall burst out with new wine (Proverbs 3: 9-10).

Thou shalt make thy prayer unto him, and he shall hear thee, and thou shalt pay thy vows. Thou shalt also decree a thing, and it shall be established unto thee: and the light shall shine upon thy ways (Job 22:27-28).

KEY STATEMENT: Maximizing our money involves the right financial confessions about the promised entitlement of increase as a result of our giving.

Contrary to popular opinion, the faith process is not complete when giving takes place; obedience simply entitles one to the promises which must be possessed by faith. All the promises of God are received by faith. After I opened up in my finances, I began to release my faith with a faith confession because, as we discovered in a previous chapter, faith is released by the words of the mouth. I have included the following financial faith confession to help you maximize your money through the giving and receiving principle.

FINANCIAL INCREASE FAITH CONFESSION

Father, I agree with Your plan for money in my life. Your Word declares that there is a seed potential in my righteous giving. Thank You, Father, that I can target my giving toward specific promises in Your Word. I choose to be a "Seed-Faith Giver" and tap into the supernatural provisions You have made available for me. I choose to applaud the success of others with no malice, envy, jealousy, or disdain. I have sown my seed for the specific promise, and I now choose with this confession to make a demand on the increase potential of my financial seed. I am a tither and a giver of seed-faith offerings; therefore, creative ideas, solutions to problems, and the willingness of others to help me abound in my life. What good thing I make happen for others, You have promised to make happen for me. I am excited at every opportunity to make a vow and pay it, because my seed of obedience sets in motion the answer to the financial lack in life and the day of trouble that could be in my future. I boldly declare that my financial seed causes me to be sustained in difficult times. I rejoice to give because what I sow today secures my tomorrow. I have sown a righteous seed for victory in difficult relationships and the deliverance of others I love. Go, ministering spirits,

and cause my faith expectations to come to pass! I call it forth now! Peace, Love, and Joy, come to me! Increase, come to me! In Jesus' name, Amen.

CONCLUSION

Although it is clear from the Word of God that He wants us to prosper, to overcome adversity, and to succeed, many will hear and understand such teachings but will never rise to the place of action. Annually, I host a Church Development Strategies Conference where thousands of pastors and their key leaders gather for several days of intensive strategizing for church growth. What is so exciting about this ministry to churches is that the excitement generated at the conference becomes action on their home front as they implement the strategies.

The entire effort of writing this book and bringing you into my huddle to share with you the principles of maximizing life will be an exercise in futility unless you apply what you have learned. It would be tragic to go to a football game knowing that your team had spent the week in preparation for the contest, but your team never shows up on the playing field. There comes a time in life when you must make good on time spent in preparation. You get no credit for the time you spent preparing for the game if you never leave the locker room and actually play the game.

As you may have noticed, several principles were repeated throughout this book for clarity. It is through repetition that learning takes place.

I sincerely believe that you have the potential to do much more, to accomplish much more, and to experience greater productivity and fulfillment. It's time to quit watching others excel in life and celebrate their success while your vision for a better life remains an unfulfilled dream. This book is designed to do for you what a friend did for me when I was a teenager because he saw potential in me. I think it's good to close the book with this story of a friend of mine who helped me stretch beyond my comfort zone to achieve success.

I grew up in the ghetto, and we did not have private swimming pools in our backyards. If we wanted to experience a refreshing swim, we had to go to the neighborhood swimming pool provided by the city. It was always crowded at the neighborhood pool, which was divided into two sections, the shallow end and the deep end. Of course, the shallow end was always more crowded than the deep end because it was the section of the pool for the non-swimmers and beginners.

When my friend and I went to the pool, he was a good swimmer and went immediately to the deep end where there were fewer swimmers and more room to enjoy the swimming experience. I was not that good, so I went to the shallow section that was crowded with hardly any room to enjoy the day. It was so crowded I could barely take a few swimming strokes before I bumped into someone. After offering apologies I attempted to swim again, if someone did not bump into me. It was both a frustrating and a refreshing experience; after all, I was at the park and in the cool water of the swimming pool.

Occasionally, I looked over at the deep end section where the

swimmers looked as though they were having the time of their lives. The diving board was in the deep end, and I saw them leap from the diving board into the water and come up surrounded by a ball of bubbles. There was so much room there that the swimmers could swim unobstructed. Wow!

One day my friend told me that he had been watching me swim and that he really thought I could swim in the deep end of the pool. I was most cautious and shocked at the thought of swimming in the deep end without the security of my feet being able to touch the bottom of the pool at will. He continued to express his confidence and convinced me that I could pass the test that would qualify me as a deep-end swimmer. The test was to swim across the pool and back under the watchful eye of the lifeguard. If I completed the swim to the lifeguard's satisfaction, I qualified to swim in the deep end. My friend comforted me even more by assuring me that he would run along side the pool while I was taking my test to encourage me and to rescue me if I needed help.

Because of his confidence and motivation, I agreed. I went to the lifeguard and expressed my desire to take the swimmer's test and he agreed. He blew his whistle; the shrieking sound alerted all swimmers that someone was about to take the test and the waterway was cleared. All eyes were on me and, with the coaching of my friend, I was ready! The next time the lifeguard blew the whistle, which signaled the start of the test, I dived into the water and began stroking. I could hear my friend's encouragement as the water rushed past my ears. With my heart pumping fast, I kept stroking until I reached the other side of the pool.

My friend had taught me how to flip and to push off the other side to maximize my momentum. The flip went well and I was on my

way back to the other side; the test was half completed. My arms were getting tired, my kick was getting weaker, and the thought of quitting began ringing in my head; but I could hear my friend telling me that I was almost there, not to quit now. "One stroke at a time," he yelled! "One stroke at a time!" I consented and kept stroking; my second wind came, my kick got stronger, and I knew I was about to touch the bank. I had passed the test, and now I was deep-water qualified!

The crowd of onlookers began to cheer, and my friend jumped up and down in celebration. It was an incredible experience. Now, I could really enjoy the pool while swimming in the deep water! Thank God my friend saw deep-water potential in me.

What this simple story is conveying to you, my friend, is that I believe every person who picks up this book and reads it has deep-water potential. No, not to physically swim in the deep end of a pool. Deep-water potential suggests that you can do more and accomplish more than you are presently doing. Like my friend who encouraged me and pushed me to perform at a higher level, this book is designed to push you to your next level of performance and productivity.

My greatest hope from this ministry through the written word is that one day I will receive correspondence from readers saying this work encouraged them to take action to maximize their situations. One day soon I hope to get emails at *maximizer@newlight.org* from readers testifying that this book provided the spark to ignite their faiths, provoked them to take responsibility for their futures, and charted a course for their successes. Until those emails arrive or the correspondence comes through the mail, I will continue to share with others the principles that have transformed my life, my mar-

riage, and my ministry. I do hope I am helping others and the maximized state I know and enjoy is being used to bless others! Remember, God created you to win in life!